HURON COU

P9-EIF-188

Don't Move!

Renovate Your House
& Make Social Contacts

Don't Move!

Renovate Your House
& Make Social Contacts

Eric Nicol

McClelland and Stewart Limited
Toronto/Montreal

0-7710-6768-2

The Canadian Publishers
McClelland and Stewart Limited
25 Hollinger Road, Toronto 374

Printed in Canada

Contents

To

Ray, Wilf, Maddin, Jim, Bruce, Guy, Bob,
the Hairy Man who helped Sam, Arthur,
Arthur #2, Alf, Max and his Mate, Mr.
Nolan, all the boys at Permanent Roofing
Insulation, Bill, the Steel Brothers, the Iron
Men, Two Unidentified Carpet Layers,
Larry, Three Rather Clique-ish Stucco
Men, and to their apprentices, wives,
girlfriends and other persons to whom we
gave the business as usual during alterations.

The Premise:
Room at the Top

My adolescent years were harried by the fear that I was impotent. I knew, in my private and continuing agony, that at the critical moment the most I'd be able to give a woman would be a thin smile.

My mother thought it was hayfever. But the reason my eyes were red and I sneezed a lot every morning was that I lay awake each night, dreading the revelation that I was a natural-born eunuch, a genealogical dead-end. I sensed that in adulthood my appropriate housing would be a carbarn because I was the end of the line.

Thirty years and three children later, impotence looks pretty good. I don't say that I would choose it as a way of life, but when you have married well into your thirties, as I did, and bought a small cottage on the assumption that nature has equipped you to provide a model for Zero Population Growth, your being the last family portrait on the wall seems a lesser evil than running out of wall to hang on.

Unexpected family growth was the motivation for our seeking larger accommodation. We had two children sleeping in the basement, and the only access to the attic was made when the noise level became such that Daddy rose through the ceiling without benefit of stairs.

Because our youngest (six) was stashed in the cellar with the sowbugs and bottles of cheap Canadian wine, the TV set had to be billeted in the living room, where it would not disturb the little fellow's struggle to find slumber in concubinage with Old Faithless (the furnace), which comes on like Krakatoa. The presence of active television and children in the living room made it difficult to entertain our guests there without:

(a) quelling the TV set, the children leaving the room with as little grace as possible and the ugly scene climaxed by a guest sitting down on the residuum of a jelly sandwich, or

(b) the children and TV staying on, the adult conversation trying to compete with the audio and gradually drying up as the intellectual tone of an evening at the Nicols' was defined by Tarzan Meets Abbott and Costello.

But don't misunderstand me, please. We did not enlarge our abode in order to expand a pretension to gracious living. My wife and I gave up our attempt at gracious living right after the neighbor's poolside party during which Myrl laughed so hard her partial plate blew out. As a bridge projected across the water it was coolly received, and it put paid to any vestige of ambition to be admitted to the local jet set.

In fairness to my wife I should point out that my own social graciousness is impaired by the habit of absently scratching my crotch, like a baseball pitcher bemused by the catcher's sign. Years of solitary composition engrain little mannerisms like this that cancel out anything gained socially from prestige housing.

Much more impelling than the demands of entertaining our own guests were those imposed by the children's friends, who liked to assemble outside my den-office door and hold a faithful reproduction of the Woodstock pop festival. Also, as they grow older, girl children have pyjama parties. In the circumstances of sharing the bathroom, and of my sleeping in the raw during summer, it was jarring to all concerned when my unscheduled flight to the facility collided with half a dozen young women, all strangers to me.

One can get only so much mileage out of the casual "Hi, there." Then the word gets around among neighbor parents that you are on the police suspect list for exposing.

Holed up in the garage to escape the moving wall of sleeping bags, I worked out a basic principle in the physics of family living: the volume of the accommodation decreases in ratio to the pressure on the bathroom.

Husband and wife can live on one plane so long as it is reasonably horizontal. But with children the ranch-style house functions only if the halls are wide enough for a quarter horse to control the herd.

Besides, my wife had always wanted a house with an upper story. This is the Anne-of-Green-Gables fixation, the feeling that life is not complete unless you can start the day by falling downstairs. With the option of ending the day by falling upstairs.

I admit that I too have envied the father who can issue pronouncements from an upstairs balcony, to offset his being the stocky type. For me the appeal of an upstairs is partly papal and, no doubt, partly vestigial from the descent from the trees that some of my critics have dated as being more recent than is indicated by evolutionary charts.

These then were our reasons for raising the roof. For you, the reader, who have clutched at this book as a straw with which to make the brick of decision, the stimulus may be quite different. Some people have to accommodate older relatives, or foundlings, or large stray animals. Occasionally a homeowner thinks that by adding another floor he can rise above the smog. (Actually there is more oxygen at ground level. Build an extension to your coldframe and throw yourself on the mercy of the celery.)

The very worst reason for renovating is resale. An astounding number of people bare their bosoms to the slings and arrows of outrageous foremen in the expectation of getting a few thousand dollars more for the house. My advice to these people is: No way. You may not have had much feeling for the house before you started the renovation, but by the time this is finished you will be so emotionally involved with it as to make Tristan and Isolde look like a high-school crush.

For our house the total elapsed time, from the first glint in Myrl's eye to the final, conclusive flutter of my cheque-book, was fourteen months. I know now why Rome wasn't built in a day: they couldn't decide on the color of the wallpaper.

Don't Move!

**Renovate Your House
& Make Social Contacts**

"Beware that it be the refor
that draweth on the chang
and not the desire of chan
that pretendeth the reform

Francis Bacon, "Of Innov:

"Why mess with it?"

Wilf McKnight, our contra

1   Measure Twice, Cut Once

The planning stage of renovating your house is staggeringly vital to the success of the project. You can hardly give the matter too much thought. Indeed if you think about it long enough the children will have grown up, or Mother will have learned to love the rest home, and you save yourself as much as $30,000.

Let me say at once however that this handbook is not for triflers. If, deep down inside, you are satisfied with the palsied piano-case you inhabit, don't flirt with ordeal. If the teeming fruit of your loins are content to be stacked in the basement like cordwood, thanks to your having embraced an obscure Oriental religion that sanctions burying alive the child that asks for its own bed, keep the faith, baby.

People who have renovated their houses voice the same assessment of the experience: "We're happy with the results, but we'd never want to go through it again." Astronauts who have been given a bad time on a lunar voyage are more willing to journey again into space than is the homeowner to repeat the ascent of eight feet to the new upstairs.

True, astronauts generally eat better, sleep better and have a fuller sex life than the homeowner and his wife during alterations. Remodelling the house also provides a wide choice of exits for the owner's departure from sanity. One owner spent eight thousand plus on his new upstairs bathroom, then found that the hot water pipe had been joined to the toilet, which when flushed steamed like the bowels of Hell.

Another owner built himself several hundred feet of sturdily fixed bookshelves that proved to be too shallow to accept anything but Penguins. Rather than rip out several weeks' work he became a collector of dirty pocket novels.

You may repeat such disasters, but more likely you will break new ground, by stepping out a window not included in the plans.

For the one thing you can expect, when renovating, is the unexpected. All contractors know this. So do most tradesmen. The architect suspects that it is true but refuses to admit it. Only Old Starry Eyes (you) enters into the agreement under the impression that modern technology has mastered man's capacity for blundering and the mysteries of Dry Rot (to say nothing of its old-soak brother, Wet Rot).

Bewildered by this costly apprehension of the unseen, as explained to me by the contractors who came to audition the house for renovation, I told anybody who would listen: "But our house was built as his own home by a contractor who spared no expense." My listeners still gave me the fish eye. As far as the trades are concerned, your house was erected by the same Jerry who built the false-front saloons for the Hollywood western.

You may have thought that the swinging doors on your front porch were a cute accent. To the trades they mark the entrance where the bad guys swaggered into a vacant lot.

Learning little facts such as these, the homeowner may revise his whole plan to renovate, in line with the structural method summarized by: Screw it.

He will likely return to the idea of getting rid of the house and buying a new one. It is not uncommon for the homeowner to vacillate for months, even years, between remodelling and moving out. I found it helpful, though not very, to list the advantages and disadvantages of the options:

Moving:

1. You will have a FOR SALE sign on your front lawn, confirming the neighborhood rumor that the mortgage payments have finally broken your back.

2. You get to meet a lot of people who come to inspect your house, sniffing at your sump, turning on all your taps at once to test the water pressure, driving small penknives into your porch posts in search of rot, etc.

3. You get to meet a lot of people by going to *their* houses, sniffing at their sump, turning on all the taps, etc.

4. You will pay the realtor up to five per cent of the price you obtain for your house. Money down the drain, but possibly the only thing the drain accepts.

5. You also pay the charge for transport of your belongings by a moving van that takes very good care of your treasures but delivers them to Akron, Ohio.

6. The change of address will throw your creditors off the scent for a few hours.

Remodelling:

1. "It will be less bother than trying to find another house." (This line, accompanied by hysterical laughter, is often repeated after the renovation, as the owner is led away to the padded van.)

2. "The divvil ye know is better than the divvil ye don't." Another popular rationale, and one that makes sense only to the Irish.

3. Your children will not suffer the psychological damage of being uprooted from school and friends. This is sound logic, unless of course your children all hate their school and have no friends, in which case the hell with them.

4. You won't have to get to know a bunch of new neighbors. Again, this depends on how well you have been getting on with your *old* neighbors. If the old neighbors have been burning a cross on your front lawn and smearing excrement on your gazebo, the chances are that the relationship will not be improved by your suddenly throwing up a superstructure that further impedes their view.

After weighing these arguments, pro and con renovation, you will find that you are that much closer to turning yourself into a gypsy fortune teller. For our family, the scales were tipped by special circumstances, such as my wife's relationship with our butcher. Our butcher understands that a writer cannot afford to buy as choice cuts of meat as those of his customers who come up from the nearby Indian reserve. He is very considerate about lending Myrl his jeweller's glass to examine the steak that is within our budget, and he doesn't complain about subdividing a sausage.

Breaking in a new butcher can be arduous, at our time of life.

Too, our present house has a quite good view overlooking the Strait of Georgia. It is a source of comfort to be able to look out the window and see that the pollution is not just local but stretches to the far horizon, wherever that is.

Offsetting the view somewhat was the fact that our house is fairly close to the Vancouver International Airport, the big jets making increasingly frequent overflights when the normal landing circuit is crowded. Elevating the roof skyward increased the likelihood of our informally hosting a Boeing 747 – and we have only six sherry glasses.

What finally decided us to renovate instead of buy, however, was my very strong, sentimental attachment to the buck. Inflated prices of houses meant that we could pay as much as $20,000 differential for a larger house that might or might not have the attractive features of the old house (view, butcher simpatico, etc.). For $20,000,

I surmised, we could have the old house transformed into a Taj Mahal with en suite bathroom. We were phantasizing again, of course, but with some excuse:

We had been reading the weekend supplement of the newspaper. In recent years home renovation has been a favored topic with the Sunday pictorials. Sort of an extension of the funnies. The remodel-your-house articles glow with color photos of the House After, which beside the black-and-white stills of the House Before look like escape from the ghetto.

Invariably Alice and Harry produced this miracle for under $6000. The author of the article concedes that at that price "Harry helped with some of the finishing." I'll bet he did. He also sold his father into slavery to the lumberyard.

One of these effulgent essays described a transformation very similar to that Myrl and I envisaged for our place: an aging bungalow capped by three new rooms, the "cheerless" downstairs hallway opened up by a stately staircase that swept down in expectation of Empress Eugenie under a chandelier grand enough to light little undying fires of envy in every neighbor within a two-block radius. All for six thousand.

We cut out the photos and scotch-taped them to one of our paint-chipped kitchen cupboards, where in the months to come it provided endless amusement for passing throngs of tradesmen.

We had our dream, in full color. All that remained was to settle on the method of realizing the vision as happily as Alice and Harry had done. Never once did it occur to us to notice that none of the photos of their renovation included a picture of the couple themselves. The reason for that of course being that Alice and Harry were both dead – on a contract to remodel their interiors.

2 Into the Wild Blueprints

And those things which have long gone together are as it were con-federate within themselves: whereas new things piece not so well; but though they help by their utility, yet they trouble by their incon-formity. (Bacon, "Of Innovations")

The one place never troubled by inconformity is the home re-modelled by the genius – he melds the more brilliant talents of Frank Lloyd Wright, Le Corbusier and whoever wrote the specifica-tions for Cloud Nine – who does the photo layout for the home-and-garden magazine, for the Modern Living section of *Life* and for similar journalistic depictions of places attainable if your old house is swept up by a tornado that deposits you and your little dog in Glossyland.

You know the photos I mean. The house is a panoply of tasteful decor. Mother lounges decoratively against the massive stone fire-place in which logs burn cleanly. In their bright and orderly rooms, the children are seen curled up with a good book, in positions that complement the arrangement of other inanimate objects. And on the sundeck, puffing smokelessly on his pipe and tranquil beyond the wildest hopes of Nembutal, stands the old man. The deck rail against which he leans is nowhere puddled with prune whip.

I can't identify.

Where, for instance, are the halves of old auto tire at corners of the hall to serve as bumpers for the kids' trikes?

I have examined the pictured chairs and chesterfields carefully, under a magnifying glass, without discerning the missing buttons, the frayed upholstery, that in our house are the personal touch of a cat that plucks as a little sign of contentment. All of our chairs and sofas have received the treatment because a cat will not sleep on a seat once it has thrown up on it.

Okay, so they have had the cat's claws pulled. Where in the living room of this excitingly designed home is the rug strewn with raffia that has leaked out of splits in the hassock? To my children a hassock is a piece of gym equipment, to be pummelled, rolled over, juggled on the feet and bounced off the ceiling. How else does a child get exercise while watching television? Show me a healthy hassock, and I'll show you a flabby kid.

Where, in the model bathroom, is the Scottie dog calendar positioned on the wall opposite the W.C. to conceal a strange type of lead-base leprosy afflicting the paint at that spot? I am accustomed to a bathroom whose ceiling is dappled with gobs of toothpaste. How the toothpaste gets up there is one of the little mysteries of family life, but we are pretty well committed to mint-flavored brands whose green does not clash with the basic candy-stripe.

It has been my experience that the heap o' living it takes to make a house a home also makes it an interior decorator's nightmare. One of us – either the homes-and-gardens editor or I – is out of touch with reality. And I don't think it's me.

Worse mischief, however, is perpetrated by the picture magazines when they encourage the homeowner to do major renovations himself. For sheer volume of damage done to body and spirit, for breakdown of family life, alcoholism, divorce and suicide, *Playboy* and the porno mags are positively benign compared to the publication that runs articles with titles like "Convert That Old Attic Into a Child's Charming Bedroom – In Your Spare Time!" Before the do-it-yourselfer finishes charming the bedroom the child will have long since grown into a full-blown delinquent and found more permanent accommodation in a house of correction.

The old adage "If you want something done right, do it yourself" holds true for certain elementary activities, such as sexual intercourse. Whether it applies to a complicated project such as adding rooms to one's house is questionable. The equally old adage "The person who acts as his own lawyer has a fool for a client" seems more pertinent, if we substitute "builder" for "lawyer," the client in both actions being apt to end up in a small, uninviting room that denies him access to the outside world.

That the do-it-yourselfer is a professional merely darkens the auspices. The painter's house is always the house that needs painting, and it is the carpenter's wife who sits rocking her rocking chair in the unfinished shell of the playroom, trying to remember what they were going to play there.

Yet I too toyed for a time with the idea of doing the renovation myself. I sent away for a booklet on the subject, the slim volume arriving in due course and proving every bit as readable as the Rosetta Stone. I was able to get the main drift of the plot – this old stud gets involved with a paint stripper and ends up plastered – but the sub-plots escaped me entirely.

One reason for this was that building supplies have odd, archaic names – *10-penny nails*, for example, which have nothing to do with the Canadian penny or indeed any penny including Henny Penny. A 10-penny nail is a nail of certain length known to carpenters, and they aren't telling. Other names for building material go back to biblical times. The clerks in lumberyards look chronically grumpy because people come in and ask for material without having first measured their house in cubits. They prefer to wait on somebody who is building an ark.

My failure to understand the build-it-yourself manual discouraged but did not surprise me. I had no previous history of competence as a handyman. A person who has taken an hour and a half to assemble the plastic helicopter his child has found in a box of Sugar Pops, and still gets the rotor blade on the underside, is not a prime prospect for finishing the attic except in the terminal sense of the word.

At school, Manual Training, as woodworking was then called, was my weakest subject. Mr. Watson, our manual-training teacher, regarded me as a scourge that God had sent down to the school basement to try his soul and, more important, his limited supply of tools. No matter what object he assigned us to make – a match-scratcher (a piece of sandpaper glued to a block of wood) or a pot-coaster (a block of wood glued to a piece of sandpaper) – all I could make was shavings. I was also big on sawdust. But the plane was my main weapon for destroying the school board's budget for instructional lumber. The more determined that Mr. Watson became that I should make a square edge, the deeper the lovely curls piled up around my ankles.

If there were such a thing as a shavings account, I would have been rich, rich, rich.

Forty years later I show the same standard of efficiency with tools. My wife learned early in our marriage that if odd jobs around the house were going to be done, she would have to do them. Her father, a fine craftsman who had worked for most of his life in wholesale hardware, shortly after his daughter married me presented me with a large metal tool case stocked with a variety of tools. He watched me soberly for fifteen minutes while I tried to figure out how to open the tool case (it had a rather tricky latch). He never gave me any more tools.

But Myrl's Dad did like to drop in from time to time to see the latest thing I had fixed with scotch tape. The way I restored the rocks fallen out of the garden wall particularly impressed him, as he had never thought of mortar in terms of old bubble gum. When I told him that I was thinking of remodelling the house myself he laughed so hard he fell off the chair – which admittedly had one leg shorter than the others.

I was further dissuaded from doing my own renovating when my wife told me about one of our neighbors, a fellow of some skill with hammer and saw, who had not yet completed the staircase he had begun several years earlier to connect the new upstairs with the downstairs. His family was now so accustomed to using the firemen's brass pole to reach the ground floor that the younger children cried when confronted by a conventional set of steps.

Another do-it-yourselfer I heard of had been working on his renovation for so many years that when he at last completed it he found that his life was empty. He had failed to develop any other hobbies, or to make any friends, or to communicate with his wife, during the latter period of his life that was devoted to fitting windows. As a result, he fell into a psychological decline that became physical, and he died the same day that his new carport collapsed.

About this time Myrl and I had recommended to us an Old Country carpenter who specialized in renovation. There is something irresistible about the carpenter advertised as Old Country. One immediately envisages the long-lived virtues of the joiner who built Shakespeare's house in Stratford-on-Avon. The complete artisan. One whose integrity is so thoroughly Anglo-Saxon that if his hammer but bends a nail, he uses his lunch hour to build a gibbet on which to hang himself.

So we grabbed at the Old Country carpenter, whom I'll call Mr. Potter. Mr. Potter turned up after work one day and gazed at our house from the street. He was dour, every bit as dour as we had hoped for. Instinctively we knew that a tradesman who has learned to smile has been working at a profit, or has otherwise done something he shouldn't. Later we were to learn that many tradesmen know that customers are lulled incautious by the dour look, and they affect a dourness that is not genuine. Glum on the outside, laughing on the inside. Pagliacci in reverse. I learned to look for the telltale laugh lines around the eyes, the lapse of the lips into upturned corners. It is no exaggeration to say that it takes years of experience to recognize the tradesman who is a bona fide Old Country grump.

Mr. Potter was the real thing. With a minimum of civility he acceded to our invitation to inspect the attic from the inside. It was clearly no thrill for him, no consummation of return to the womb, to climb into the vaginal orifice of the trapdoor in the ceiling of the hall closet. He soon reappeared as a breech delivery, covered with an after-birth of smut.

Reluctantly he admitted that there was space enough under the roof to build one room, with a small dormer window and a crawl space in case we had guests. He refused to commit himself on what this aberration would cost, but reckoned that it would be "about six thousand."

When I asked him if it would be possible to build three rooms by raising the roof like it said in the magazine, his gloom became impenetrable. The attic space was too shallow, he pointed out, for the kind of rapid roof-raising required to outwit the weather. I would need to hire a small army of midgets, all working furiously, to get the cap back on before the place was flooded out.

On this note of "Après nous, le déluge," Mr. Potter took his leave, clearly gratified by our disappointment.

Subsequent carpenters and contractors whom we called in were sunnier, most of them, till they considered raising the roof. Then the enormity of the proposition seized their tripes and they backed off. The problem was, they said, that our bungalow-style roof did not lend itself to being elevated. "If you had a gable roof it would be a piece of cake," said one. "But your roof is full of hips."

This was the first intimation we'd had that we had a hippy roof. It was chastening to learn that ours was the setting for Anne of Green Hips. Somehow it no longer sounded like a children's story.

We also discovered that a city bylaw required a minimum height of seven feet six inches at the crest of a room. This was exactly the maximum height of our attic. The city would not go along with our willingness to move from room to room on our hands and knees. We had to be able to put up a basketball player.

One contractor drew a sketch so that we could see how much more we were biting off than he could chew. The plans drawn by builders and carpenters are usually very simple affairs, conveyed on a used paper napkin or the inside of a cigaret pack. Your getting the extra bedroom depends on whether he smokes king-size.

This encourages the homeowner to make his *own* drawings of the proposed addition. If your drawing ability is anything like mine, you will quickly discover that you cannot draw a house. During this phase I made quite a number of drawings of what I intended to be our house, crayoning the proposed addition as I saw it. People who saw these admired them as rather charming studies by a preschooler who because of some physical disability had to draw with his feet. One person identified them as reproductions of the work of Van Gogh during the latter stages of his madness. Nobody recognized them as our house.

People who can draw a house are called architects. Some architects can also draw bigger buildings – high-rises and office blocks –

which on the whole are easier to draw than a house. Until I tried to draw our house I had thought that hiring an architect, for remodelling, was something of an affectation. I had heard other homeowners talk about "our architect" as though, like a long middle toe, only the better class of person had one.

The more I talked to homeowners who had designed their own renovations, or had accepted the ad hoc improvisations of the builder, the more I felt that resorting to an architect was a bit effeminate. And a writer can't be too careful.

Nevertheless most of the magazine articles I'd read did advise acquiring the services of "a professional architect." A professional architect is one who has B. Arch. behind his name. If he don't B. Arch., he don't be professional: a safe rule of thumb.

The problem is, how to get in touch with a professional architect who may be interested in your pitiful little project. Architects are listed in the Yellow Pages, true, but there is nothing to indicate whether a given architect is currently designing the national pavilion for a world's fair or is concentrating on third bathrooms. For me to phone some of the names listed under Architects would have been like my summoning Dr. Christian Barnard to perform the transplant of a geranium.

In this respect architects are comparable to lawyers, except that nearly everyone has a friend or relative who has a lawyer to whom he may be referred, whereas it is possible to live a whole lifetime without meeting anybody who knows a cheap architect.

We had reached a barrier so thorny that we were ready to give up the idea of adding rooms to the house, to seek some other solution to overcrowding, such as the adoption of a couple of our children by a Korean family. Before placing the newspaper ad in Seoul, however, I resorted to my newspaper column to make public our hunt for an architect with a feeble grasp of the value of money:

I went to my friendly neighborhood architectural institute, which turned out to be not all that friendly. After a while a girl came to find out why I was buttressing the counter. I said to her: "What do you have in the way of undistinguished architects?"

Apparently I was not the first to apply for information of this order, as she plucked from the file a mimeographed list of architects, listed alphabetically rather than by price range.

"Could you tell me," I said, "which of these is an architect who is just getting started in business, or perhaps has been defrocked for designing a health spa?"

The girl kindly ticked off a couple of names, intimating that the

*firms had been architectural consultants for the Tower of Pisa. She
also informed me that most architects charge twenty dollars an hour
just to come and look at the house, as a feasibility study.*

*"Ask him if he'll take ten bucks to come and make a hasty
judgment," I told my wife, when I got home, and persuaded her to
call one of the architects. I hoped that, since most architects were
gentlemen, a plea from a lady in distress might work on their
sympathy. Sure enough, the first architect that Myrl phoned prom-
ised to drive by the house to look at it. He must have driven by too
fast because we never heard from him again. The next architect she
phoned told her that he was sick – sick of being called by would-be
renovators wanting him to come and look at their houses on the
cheap.*

*And that is where, at our house, the matter rests. Architects just
have it too good. . . .*

The column elicited a number of letters from amateur architects
offering to remodel our house the same way they had remodelled
their own. Since none of them mentioned having a hippy roof, I was
not buoyed by the response. I gathered that for the professional
architect it was more profitable to design a skyscraper, dealing at
arm's length with the owner and avoiding the handshake of agreement sealed with peanut butter.

Then arrived a letter from a professional architect named Ray
Olsen. Mr. Olsen not only had letters after his name – "B. Archi-
tecture (Rand) MRAIC, ARIBA" – but his credentials as he listed
them were equally impressive:

"I am your man. And I must tell you that I completely understand your problem. I have long been involved with problems
such as yours – and I feel that I am now ready to offer my
services to you and thousands like you. In preparing for this
event I have made many an interesting study. I remember the
addition which Mr. and Mrs. Nero were considering. After many
long hours of discussion they really got quite fired up about it.
Unfortunately he was caught fiddling the books and the project
came to naught. . . . The accommodation problem at the Colos-
seum was an interesting challenge. I found many a resident with
his back to the wall there which made building operations rather
difficult. . . ."

The man was plainly a name-dropper, but if he was prepared to
take on the job in return for dropping my name, well, the price was
right. I invited Mr. Olsen to come and see for himself whether the

31

proposed amelioration would be as challenging for him as "the Islamic arched post and beam creation" he devised for N. Bonaparte. On this bantering note began the relationship that was to lay bare my soul, warts and all.

3   The Gentle Inquisition

The architect came to tea. The minute my wife ushered him into our battle-fatigued foyer I knew that I was in deep. Mr. Olsen was six foot two. (I am five foot nine and three quarters, in a tight collar.) Mr. Olsen had a beard and the craggy good looks of Gregory Peck with perhaps a dash of Richard Burton. (I am more the Eddie Fisher type – a lovable, clean-shaven loser.) Mr. Olsen spoke with a cultured English accent. His tall, tweedy grandeur filled the entrance hall with an air of authority and thorough-going competence that utterly belied the facetiousness of his letter. Here was an architect who would not work just for laughs. I felt the sudden elevation of him who is hoist by his own petard.

Over the teacups I recognized further evidence of the professional man, of the surgeon who tells you a little joke before he amputates your leg, of the barrister whose quips preface his reading of the will of your wealthy aunt who has left everything to her parrot.

We were feeling one another out. This is standard procedure for the first meeting of architect and client. The architect knows that he can cope with your freaky hips. What he is concerned about, at this stage, is not so much the character of your structure as the structure of your character. Some people just do not have the moral foundation required for renovation. They think that they can put a sundeck on their psyche without renewing the foundation of their id.

I decided to be completely honest with Mr. Olsen. I let him see at once that my whole personality was a crawl space. The facade normally seen by our guests I let drop, revealing the Real Me.

Mr. Olsen made a brief note in his notebook and turned his attention to Myrl. The Real Me was a bit miffed at this response to my letting it all hang out. Not that I do much better when I keep it all reeled in.

However, it turned out that the architect was saving the full examination of the Real Us for another afternoon when he had more time to probe. In fact, he told us, he would need about three hours to conduct the interview to establish the family dynamics that would dictate the remodelling of our house.

Well, this was more like it. It was with a sense of true beginning that I watched lengths of Mr. Olsen rise through the trapdoor into the attic. My wife was ready to go up with him – without using the ladder. I was able to limit the miracle to a tablelamp, with which Mr. Olsen reconnoitred the enemy.

For a good many minutes Myrl and I listened to the measured tread pacing the joists, overhead, a feat of acrobatics in itself. On the night of Hurricane Frieda, October 1962, which ripped off our shingles and dumped the deluge through the exposed room, I had boosted my wife into the attic because her feet were more prehensile than mine for gripping the joists. She promptly put her foot through the hall ceiling. This solved the problem of where the water would run off, but I couldn't remember when I had less enjoyed the sight of a shapely leg.

For some reason I expected Mr. Olsen to descend from the attic as a smaller man, possibly aged considerably as well. But his tall cool was not in the least diminished. Three rooms upstairs were entirely feasible, he said, and the roof could be raised by a couple of normal-sized men rather than by a battalion of dwarfs seconded from Snow White. Elated, we agreed to the date of the next appointment – carefully recorded in the notebook – and Mr. Olsen drove away in his VW bus.

At this point I can hardly stress too firmly, dear renovator, that you must establish an honest relationship with your architect. Lie to your lawyer and your doctor if you will, but never humbug your architect. Your architect must be privy to the most intimate facts of your home life. He is a psychiatrist for whom you use your own couch. He is a priest, and your living room is the confessional wherein you spill the beans, blow the gaffe and tell it like it is, baby.

If your daughter is sharing her room with a young man she brought home one day from the community college, admit that you need a larger laundry room.

If your nights are made hideous by insomnia caused by your wife's snoring, there is no point in blabbing to your physician, but your architect should know. He can design separate bedrooms without making it look like a division of community property, or at least assign you a vibrating bed that masks the shock waves radiating from the kip adjacent.

On the morning of The Interview I showered and put on clean underwear. Not that I really believed that the architect's research into my living habits would include a physical examination. I just hoped that I wouldn't be required to pee into a bottle. I hadn't peed into a bottle since World War Two, and a man's aim doesn't improve with age.

My wife had the house spotless. The tea-tray was set with our best china. Myrl had baked some goodies* that were tasty without being ostentatious (see Appendix A, recipe for Architect's English Tea Scones). We summoned the children together and briefed them on the importance of replying to Mr. Olsen's questions truthfully and without picking their noses. We locked the cat in the storage room, a precaution against the animal's excessively cordial habit of jumping into the lap of a guest and plucking his privates.

Such was the state of readiness, that afternoon in March when Mr. Olsen returned to our house. Spring had unlocked the daffodils, but our living-room windows were still stuck. A peculiarity of our house, which is about thirty years old, is that, like other elderly beings, its joints seize up in wet weather. Because of this resistance of windows and doors to opening, I have worked out a procedure, in the event of fire, that calls for all the members of the family to assemble in the middle of the house so that we can burn to death in one another's arms.

During his unhurried detachment of the buckles of his briefcase, Mr. Olsen disclosed that he was not English but South African, recently emigrated from that country as a liberal whose views were at odds with the racist regime. He was in the process of becoming established in Canada, after an extensive practice in Johannesburg.

Now that the work he supervised is done, it is curious to reflect that one reason the addition blends so well with the original is that there was no attempt at integration in a land 12,000 miles distant from our lot.

Chatting with the children, our architect established their hobbies, their attitudes towards sunshine and shade, their traffic patterns in the house. As a father who sometimes has difficulty remembering their ages, I was astounded at the variety of their interests. They sat revealed as, well, dammit, almost like real people.

Mr. Olsen filled several pages of his notebook with the children, then turned to me. As I filled in the details of my work and leisure activities – largely a matter of moving from the brown chair to the red chair or vice versa – my life became clearly delineated.

The picture was that of a vegetable.

It was a toss-up whether I needed Mr. Olsen or the Jolly Green Giant.

---

* It is extremely doubtful that any major renovation should be attempted unless the owner can prepare goodies, or is married to someone who can prepare goodies. Although it may be possible to remodel on the strength of bought buns, the cost is often doubled and the work finished more quickly than is compatible with good craftsmanship.

One reason why our children were so polite to Mr. Olsen was that, aside from their grandparents, he was the first guest they had seen in the living room since the winter of the big snow, which trapped a brush salesman. The rigors of family life, and my working at home, had so disjoined us from our friends that it was common gossip among the neighbors that we had a body buried in the basement.

Mr. Olsen turned next to my wife. His exhaustive questioning of her rather disturbed me. The tentative plan was for a new study for me, with a bathroom and a master bedroom upstairs, and downstairs a new kitchen sink for my wife. It shook me to hear her confess, under cross-examination, that she would really like a room of her own, for sewing, for doing household accounts, and for meditating.

"You never told me you had a craving to meditate," I said, with a taut smile. A man has to call in an architect to find out that he is married to the Mahareshi.

If anything, Mr. Olsen spent more time exposing Myrl's hidden depths than he had in establishing that I was a mouldy fig. My wife kept pouring him cups of tea, and he kept drinking them, as though all her frustrations were being released through the teabag. When at last he packed up his copious notes and took his leave, he had quizzed us well past the dinner hour. I was ready to believe, with Le Corbusier, that a house is a machine for living, because I had been given the gears.

4   The Dimensions of Cloudland

Great was the excitement the day Mr. Olsen's preliminary sketches arrived in the mail. In the struggle to be the one to open the big brown envelope I good-naturedly stomped one of the children while trying to free my hand from the jaws of our youngest.

The sketches were actually very full drawings. We had no trouble identifying not only the three new rooms upstairs but also the three bedrooms that the architect had created out of the two downstairs – "so that the children can be together as a social unit" – as well as the conversion of my old den into a work centre for Myrl, by knocking down the wall that separated it from the kitchen and equipping it with a TV set and an easy chair for meditation.

In addition Mr. Olsen had created a pass-through from kitchen to dining-room so that Myrl could serve meals there without having to negotiate the swinging door (which I'd always thought of as a fun thing). More, he had projected a sundeck from the dining room that overrode my prize rhododendron.

More yet, at the terminus of Myrl's new counter and sink he had made a place to park her portable dishwasher, in her laundry room had designed three laundry bins large enough to store dirty socks for a whole division of letter carriers, and in the basement had created a music room. (Myrl plays the piano. I play the stock market.)

Finally, he had removed the cornices from the living room and dining room ceilings, replacing them with wooden beams so that the interior of the house would match the style of the exterior. As tactfully as possible Mr. Olsen had conveyed to us the fact that our house was an architectural mongrel. The outside was humble English cottage, roses rambling rustically, suggestive of Anne Hathaway before she became involved. A step inside the front screen door, however, the mood changed abruptly to Moorish seraglio (arched portals) with a touch of late Georgian prig (the fluted cornices). The exterior of the house clearly disapproved of the interior, notably the living room. The architect was trying to pull the house together. I gathered that he wanted to make it one hundred per cent simple, to capture the spirit of the inmates.

This is the Golden Hour of renovation. The architect's preliminary drawings are the dream full blown. Your house has not only had its face lifted – its entire physique has been rejuvenated from a Phyllis Diller to a Raquel Welch.

At this point the matter of total cost has not arisen. The architect has provided you, as a beginning, with the best of all possible worlds. And it is foolish not to enjoy the view before subsiding to contact with the earth.

Regretfully, anticipating that it would distend our budget of $10,000, at our next meeting with Mr. Olsen I suggested that we eliminate Myrl's work centre and instead make my old den the third bedroom for the children. The look exchanged between my wife and the architect made me feel like one of the fathers of apartheid. Mr. Olsen fought for my wife's right to meditate, his gallantry winning my grudging admiration. We moved her meditation all over the house, upstairs and down, in a see-saw battle worthy of Douglas Fairbanks Jr. or, for that matter, Sr. Mr. Olsen slashed a chandelier and tossed out several beams (ornamental) in defence of Myrl's work centre, but I subdued him with a series of lunges into the estimates.

I did not emerge from the engagement unscathed. I lost my den's private washroom, which would have enabled me to spend a penny without first making a public appearance on the stairwell balcony as Romeo bent on an unromantic mission.

Having thus compromised his sketches into the first full set of drawings, Mr. Olsen asked us what type of contract we wished him to prepared for the builder. The two most common forms of agreement – each in its own way as secure as playing Russian roulette – are the fixed-sum (or backstop) and the cost-plus. The cost-plus is also called the open-end, as in stepping into an open elevator shaft without first ascertaining the number of floors to the bottom.

I had my heart set on a fixed-sum contract. Like every other homeowner planning to renovate I was familiar with the Gothic tale of horror revolving around The Exceeding of the Estimate.

"You can add at least twenty-five per cent to the estimate," I was told again and again. The two things of which a man may be reasonably sure in this world are that night will follow day and that he can add twenty-five per cent to the estimate.

This provided me with an astral fix of sorts till I talked with a renovator who had, in his reckoning, added twenty-five per cent to the contractor's estimate, and the final cost was twenty-five per cent higher than *the combined figures*. In other words, no matter how many times you add twenty-five per cent to the estimate you will be short by twenty-five per cent.

Another hazard of the cost-plus agreement is that it is usually an informal affair omitting such highly pertinent factors as time limit for the work and guarantees against faulty workmanship.

The butterfly-like fickleness of tradesmen in flitting from job to job, before the first is complete, is one of the less entrancing phenomena of nature. The standard procedure is for the workman to begin your job and, as soon as it has reached the point of no return, to vanish, not to reappear till the moon is of a particular fullness and Venus is in the house of Taurus.

Not uncommonly a contractor will spread his crew over two or three jobs concurrently. Their presence on site then depends on the ancient principle of engineering: The wheel that squeaks loudest gets the grease. Being notoriously weak in the squeak – I have difficulty commanding the attention of headwaiters, budgies and most other forms of life – I was anxious to have the contractor locked into a timetable as iron-clad as could be forged without involving the services of a blacksmith.

My other phobia, hardly less virulent, was that, on the day following my paying the last bill, the paint would peel away from the new woodwork, the stucco would fall off, the shiplap would spring into strange, pagoda shapes, and I would be left sitting exposed to weeping skies, the cheque stubs gradually going soggy in my lifeless grasp. I beseeched the architect to seal us with small print.

It is part of the architect's job to draw up the type of contract you wish to circulate among likely contractors. This is a good thing because, drawing up his own letter of agreement, even the most cautious of homeowners is apt to omit such conditions as the contractor's obligation to remove all rubbish (your old house) and handle workmen's compensation (you want no blood on your hands but your own).

The formal contract also stipulates whether the sub-trades are to be hired and paid by the contractor or by the homeowner through his architect. As a rule it is preferable to leave the hiring to the contractor, who has established his own lines of communication with various tradesmen on previous projects.

If you have an honest and reliable builder he will bring in sub-trades that are honest and reliable. If you get a crooked contractor, or a green contractor who lets his fingers do the walking through the Yellow Pages when sub-contracting, you will watch an extended parade of gents whose last structural employment was pouring concrete around somebody's feet. It is not always easy to detect the tainted strain of sub-contracting, but generally speaking it is a bad sign when a workman removes the Dunromin or Chez When sign on your gate and replaces it with Cosa Nostra.

Nevertheless Mr. Olsen boggled – and he didn't boggle easily – at the stringency of the clauses I wanted him to write into the contract. He pointed out that the hold-back period, whereby fifteen per cent of the tradesman's bill is delayed till the homeowner is satisfied that the work has been completed to specifications, was normally for thirty days rather than for the rest of my lifetime or two hundred years, whichever came first.

I conceded this point. I also agreed to the architect's fee of ten per cent of the total cost of construction. An architect may be prepared to accept less than ten per cent, depending on how desperate he is for work. His taking anything less than seven per cent is, however, grounds for investigating his credentials. He probably got his academic degree by taking a correspondence course from Tinkertoy, Inc.

Even at ten per cent the architect is working for something very like coolie wages, on the basis of hours put in. He supervises every stage of construction and has to be on call at those moments when the will to survive flags in both you and your wife and you try to use the sample of solar bronze window glass to slash your wrists.

He also bolsters your resolve in calling for bids from non-union contractors. Union contractors are the bigger outfits that employ union tradesmen, who are usually more expensive than the independents. If you yourself are a stout union man, your employing a non-union crew may mean wrestling with your conscience. A member of the Association of Canadian Television and Radio Artists, I found that the best way to wrestle with my conscience was to fight dirty.

I did this by calling the family together and asking the members to vote on making our house an open or a closed shop. The family not only voted for the open shop, they wanted it to sell candy.

The ethical problem thus democratically solved, I gave the architect the green light to invite bids from small contractors whom he knew to be reliable. The trick was to engage a contractor whose rugged individualism, whose immoderate appetite for hard work, made him spurn the regulations and featherbedding of unionism.

In the months following I was to meet and live with so many rugged individualists that I began to talk a little like John Wayne myself. My wife swears that my legs weren't that bowed before we started renovating. And my learning to roll a cigaret with one hand would have made more sense, she said, if I smoked.

It took the rugged individualists a while to respond to Mr. Olsen's call for bids. The fixed-sum contract requires the contractor to be careful not to underestimate the cost, as he is locked into the figure he has agreed to, and can increase this only by throwing himself on the mercy of old True Grit. For this reason, builders do make house calls.

Even if it were physically feasible to take your house to his office, the builder would come to your home because he knows that he and you are going to be living together for several months, an intimate relationship compared to which his mistress is but a shape that passes in the night.

He will see more of your wife than he will of his own.

He will have less contact with his own children than with yours.

He will share with you moments of physical hardship and severe anguish, such as his sitting on a shingle-nail.

Because of these conditions of employment it is very important for the homeowner to make a favorable impression on the builder. Attention to detail cannot be stressed too strongly. For instance, a builder will drop in without warning, to get a look at the family before it has time to put on a happy face. He is adept at recognizing synthetic bonhomie and marital discord that has been spackled over for his benefit.

Because the builder, and indeed all the trades, work from 8 a.m. to 5 or 6 p.m., you can expect them to come to assess the job at hours outside the normal working day. During the period of prospective visit by the builder, therefore, it is good policy for the mother of the family to be up every morning, including weekends, at 6 a.m., her hair done and teeth in, and dressed in a duster or housecoat more attractive than the one in which she would ordinarily make the porridge. It may take a lot out of her, hobbling around the house in high heels and Geisha costume, but the sooner she rousts the kids off to school the better. They should take their lunch to school, if not their dinner.

In fact, with regard to your children, if your planning is sufficiently long-range you won't have any. Children tend to get in the way once work starts, and some contractors have had unhappy experiences with them, such as having their power saw sabotaged, or finding a gerbil in their lunch bucket. You may want to put the children into a boarding school for the duration, or find them a foster home, or, if you have the means of blackmail, force the grandparents to take them in. At the very least, bribe the children to obey you in the presence of the builder during his first visit.

Mother should also have the coffee pot on twenty-four hours a day. This is good training for the time of actual renovation. Indeed if you are really serious about signing a contract you will invest early in a commercial, restaurant-type coffee urn, the type that serves a hundred cups without blinking. You may also wish to consider importing your coffee beans in bulk from Colombia.

Do *not* consider, even momentarily, serving a builder or tradesman instant coffee, instant tea, or instant anything except instant money. What he really enjoys, as a rugged individualist, is *boiled* coffee, cooked over an open campfire and served in an old chipped enamel mug in a setting of primordial splendor. The least you can do is serve him good perked coffee with a pine cone stuck in your ear.

Come to think of it, Mother had better get up at 5 a.m. She will need to do a good deal of baking. Builders are usually big men, and are often on a diet at home. This means that they need food that is nourishing and rich but low in calories because your wife lies about it. Carpenters, on the other hand, are always lean people. They enjoy a snack that is fattening for anybody else. (See Appendix A, recipes for Builder's Cherry Bars and Carpenter Coffee Cake.)

Warning: don't overdo it with the first impression. Avoid setting too high a standard, one that you are unable to sustain when the going gets tough. The builder wants to see more than a pretty face and petit-fours. There is no point, for instance, in Mother's looking like a Vegas showgirl if she is going to disintegrate over the long haul – and I use the word *haul* in the literal sense. The builder knows that he will need domestic slaves capable of carrying, each, a cardboard box filled with eighty pounds of rubble at least sixty feet over piles of lumber. If you have a bad back, you should make it known to the contractor that this in no way impairs the lifting capacity of your wife/husband or (if she lives with you) your mother-in-law. (Note: physical conditioning of the homeowner is discussed more fully in Chapter 9, section IV "Other tools," but it is never too early to consider the possibility that you simply do not have a constitution strong enough to survive the surgery on your domicile.)

Despite our putting our best collective foot forward, and evolving a cup of coffee too thick to stir and too thin to plough, only two rugged individualists showed up to look at our house. Both submitted bids in excess of $20,000, based on a system of calculation unrelated to the drawings.

Not only did this cause me to fumble my makin's but my legs were straightened.

Luckily, the setback was only temporary. The architect explained that one reason for the unexpectedly high estimates was the inclusion by the contractor of the "scare factor."

"Shucks," I said, still a little unsteady as I remounted for the return to Marlboro country, "what's a scare factor?"

Mr. Olsen explained that the scare factor was an amount, usually $1000, that the contractor added to his estimated costs as a hedge against encountering the unpredictable. From the totals of the tenders we had received I gathered that with our house the scare factor amounted to sheer terror.

The basic estimate seemed enough to cover anticipation of every eventuality except finding a live buffalo lodged between the joists. Added to this was the intimation that, from their examination of our attic, the contractors had found so much potential of hidden problems that they had to be put under sedation before they would bid at all.

When they removed the insulation they would find that the ceiling was suspended from a few strands of used chicklet, which had lost more than its flavor. I now understood why one of the contractors had remarked that when he stood in the attic the belching of termites, though discreet, was ubiquitous.

The chance being minimal of our reducing the scare factor by an appreciable degree of fright, we returned to the drawing-board, eliminating the sundeck and the cast-iron bathtub, and resigning ourselves to an interior that belied the exterior.

Scrubbing the tub was the part that hurt. For the new bathroom upstairs Myrl and I, and especially I, had our hearts set on a cast-iron tub because the ordinary steel tub is not built to cradle the back. Incredible though it seems, bathtub manufacturers have not, as of this writing, developed a steel tub contoured so that the bather can lie back without dislocating the upper vertebrae.

Not only does the cast-iron tub cost twice as much as a steel tub, but because it weighs a young ton every contractor who looked at our plans blanched and groaned: "Cast-iron tub." Mr. Olsen explained that the problem was that it was impossible to place the tub in the bathroom before the bathroom was built, but once the bathroom had been framed in the contractor faced a labor of Hercules to bull the tub up to the bathroom. Part of the scare factor was apprehension that a runaway tub would result in wall-to-wall carpenter. Given a choice, the contractor would prefer to install any other kind of vessel short of aircraft carrier.

Having apprised us of these facts of life in the raw, our architect told me to blow my nose and be a little man about taking Myrl and me to a bathroom display centre, there to find fulfilment in the revealed wonders of ablution, ex Suburbia.

47

5   Cleanliness Is Next to Costliness

Few thoughts are more disturbing than this: at the moment in man's evolved history when he is loping confidently about the lunar surface, he is still slipping in his bathtub. It is more than symbolic that astronaut John Glenn, after surviving orbital flights, racked up his sacroiliac while stepping out of the tub in his own home. If anything needs help from Houston Control, it is a man during splashdown in his tub.

The bathtub is the one major creature comfort that has retrogressed in both design and performance. The 19th century was the tub's heyday, when the sturdy six-foot hull stood four-square and hip high on its great iron feet. Today, because the bathroom has been effeminated, the tub is tucked prettily into a corner to make room for the vanity and other fancies.

For the male, it was game over when he was sent to the shower.

This has happened in North America, the Big Country. In smaller lands the people bathe more spaciously, the Japanese even spreading themselves to mixed doubles in their dipping, yet we in this vast territory must fold ourselves into dinky, shallow shells that are a travesty of proper accommodation for soaking, ruminating, playing with one's rubber duck, and other activities that reassemble the shattered nerves. American know-how has brought us to this, a man pretzeling his length into a sawed-off sarcophagus.

If a man is built lanky his limbs are jackknifed so that he looks like a praying mantis afflicted by agnostic doubts. Even those of us politely referred to as "stocky" require room for the expansive thoughts generated by "the benison of hot water." As a writer I can testify that I have had some of my finest ideas while steeped in the tub, the best of them being the idea of staying in another ten minutes.

I have a theory about the bathtub scenes that have been the bread-and-butter ploy of Hollywood epics. I believe that what makes these scenes enticing to men is not so much the cupcake sudsing in the nude as the ample dimensions of her tub. On the late-late movie the other night I saw Hedy Lamarr luxuriating in a tub that must have been at least a 94-55-63, including faucets. Enough to drive a man crazy with desire.

Outsize beds we have. Why not bathtubs tailored for long

thoughts? If they are truly interested in helping the submerged majority (men), bathroom designers should look to the Baths of Caracalla. Measure them. Make casts of them. Emulate them. For, say what we may about the decline of the Roman Empire, those people knew how to lave.

All of this I knew before Myrl and I visited the bathroom display centre. But we were under orders from the architect to go to the centre and choose the bathtub, basin and biffy that were Us. He refused to impose on us his taste in sanitary appointments, despite my pleading with him to be dogmatic about the magazine photos that ranged in style from Turkish seraglio to contemporary, hard-line cut-and-run.

Myrl and I entered the bathroom display centre tentatively, awed by the fluted columns, the tactful play of waters, the sheer *gleam* of font and pedestal. Everything looked so good I just didn't know where to sit.

A smartly groomed young woman manifested herself from among the marble basins. Could she help us?

"We'd like to see something in a toilet," I blurted.

My wife took over our end of the conversation following the one-minute silence observed out of respect for the passing of my foot into my mouth.

We looked at vanities. Vanitas, vanitatum, all is over two hundred bucks. In the mirrors I looked healthier than I did in the bathroom mirror at home, till I looked at the price tag. Then it was old Don Knotts again, staring back at me haggard and flinching.

I wandered off by myself, among the enclosures displaying various elegant ensembles of bathroom furnishings. Twiddling the gold-plated plungers, I recalled latrines I had known: in the student hostel in Paris the dark shaft in the corner of an unlit corridor, bottomless, bladder-freezing; the Arab toilet (two steel footplates facing Mecca) in Damascus; the English Gothic overhead job with the chain-pull in the London rooming-house ("the Pit and the Pendulum" we residents called it). My, going has come a long way.

Despite their svelte lines and pastel hues, the tubs looked as incommodious as I had anticipated. I climbed into one, and was testing the one hundred per cent horizontal position when the hostess and my wife appeared around the corner. I sprang out, stepping into the bidet.

"Refreshing," I said, "after a hot bath."

Impassive, the two women moved onto the row of johns arranged in ascending order of sportiness. I dogged along, close enough to overhear the price being quoted for the top of the line, a low-profile model both noiseless and odorless. It was so expensive that the owner would find it prohibitive to have an attack of constipation.

My wife noted the name and number of a more standard type – decibel output somewhere short of the Rainbow Falls, Niagara – and of a tub with a tread etched on the bottom to obviate the need of a bathmat.

"You don't have a re-tread, I suppose?" I was saying, as my wife pushed me out the door.

We'd had our look at the symbol of America's decadent materialism, but, damn, we couldn't afford it.

The architect received our selection of plumbing with his usual polite inscrutability. Thorough-going, he showed us a booklet illustrating hardware to accompany the porcelain, and gently nudged us towards the more utilitarian knobs and plugs. This proved to be unnecessary, as the plumbers installed what they happened to have in stock.

Mr. Olsen also drew our attention to the need to choose tile for the tub enclosure. A wide variety of substances are available for enclosures, from marble and waterproofed teak to Arborite and a plastic mold that includes the tub itself. This unibody construction makes the tub safer in the event of collision with another vehicle, but is otherwise uninviting. As our bathroom was to be well above ground level, we decided to tempt fate by staying with tile. There is nothing like good, old-fashioned tile (made in Japan) for giving a cold shower that extra touch of austerity.

We were nervous about falling headlong into hedonism because Mr. Olsen had specified rose-tinted glass for the bathroom window. I associated stained glass with Chartres. The trade name for the rosy, obscurant glass is in fact "cathedral." I wasn't sure whether we were installing a toilet or the world's shortest pew. Later, I was to be immensely grateful to the pink light for giving my naked flesh, reflected in the mirror, the semblance of active circulation.

At these moments – and they will be many before your renovation is done – the only course is to have faith. In God, if possible, but in your architect, definitely.

51

6   Enter, the Builder

The second wave of contractors to whom the architect distributed the scaled-down drawings were ones whose work he was necessarily less familiar with. One or two, when they arrived to inspect the proposition, struck me as being not only just off the boat but still under the influence of dramamine.

The phenomenon here is that the building trades are the large importers of labor from Europe – mostly Germans, Dutch, Italians, or Britons from the smaller, peripheral isles where the Celtic tongue has not changed much since the time when the natives smeared themselves with blue vegetable dye to deter the Romans by setting up a woad block. It takes only a few months, apparently, for the more industrious of the immigrants to graduate to bossing their own construction outfit. The communication gap remains measurable, however, and we faced up to the possibility of having to translate all specifications to the metric system, if not providing accommodation for an interpreter during the renovation.

One contractor who vaulted the language barrier straight into our attic descended almost immediately, nodding his admiration of the architect's drawings while holding them upside down.

Another arrived with an English-speaking appraiser who calculated the cost of the materials while the contractor engaged me in a halting but heated harangue on biculturalism. As a native of Norway he resented the prospect of having to learn French as well as English. Seeing his assistant standing by, pencil poised, I made a point of deploring Quebec's demand for special status in the ethnic mosaic that is the nation. His bid was still over $17,000, which meant that we had not succeeded in screening off the French doors to the dining room.

The second wave of contractors ebbed without floating our dreamboat. Six months, including the summer of good building weather, had passed, and I had nothing to show for our efforts except the architect's drawings and his receipt for the four hundred dollar advance on his fee (calculated on the basis of three instalments of the ten per cent of the new projected cost of $12,000). It looked very much as though we had shot the price of an air ticket to Hawaii on a set of sketches that would return the investment only if Mr. Olsen proved to be another Leonardo.

Then one day in November I went to the barber shop. I had

been to the barber shop before, as it happened. To the same barber. In fact Paul has been cutting my hair for twenty years and is more familiar with my personal problems than are members of my immediate family. We had of course discussed the renovation of my house many times, and I had his approval, in principle, to go ahead with it.

More important, his customers included a number of other homeowners who had renovated their houses. Paul made a point of remarking, in their presence, on my wandering in the wasteland in search of a contractor. They in turn volunteered a description of their own work, as well as their judgment of the builder who did it.

Now, it is important to understand that the barber shop is one place where men meet in an atmosphere of honest communication. I cannot say whether the same holds true for women in a beauty shop, but in the tonsorial chair, or seated waiting for it with his honest men's magazine open to a page of simple truths, a man lets his hair down.

The barber shop matches the candor of the pub without the blurring of detail that sometimes deranges information exchanged over a glass. A man never lies to another man sitting in the barber chair because the latter is already too vulnerable, a sitting duck-cut, so to speak.

From the surprising number of fellow patrons who had remodelled their homes I was able to make up a file of names of builders, with comments of the clients. It meant having a haircut more often than I would have done otherwise (once a month), but it was money well spent. If your house is going to have a new upstairs, you must expect to lose a little off the top. Often.

It was from one of the shorn that I heard an enthusiastic endorsement of builder Wilf McKnight. Paul the barber also recommended Mr. McKnight, having cut his hair for many years, thus keeping a complete dossier on the McKnight Construction Company.

"A good man," said Paul. "Builds big, solid houses. Works on the job himself. Nothing better than to have the boss right there on the job. Comb it wet or dry?"

The next time that Paul had the McKnight Construction Company in his chair he gave it a hot towel and my phone number. Mr. McKnight called me, and we arranged for him to visit the house with his carpenter-lieutenant, Maddin MacLeod. Both lived only a few blocks from our house and had been residents of the area for as long as I had (forty years).

54

It was a case of travelling the world in search of the perfect woman, and finally finding that she was the girl next door.

The solidly-built McKnight and his wiry partner spent more time sizing up our attic than had all the other contractors combined. After their second lengthy examination they reappeared from the loft to announce with quiet satisfaction that one of the drawings was out six inches, in the wall of a cupboard.

I knew that I had my men.

Anybody that conscientious about proving an architect wrong was obviously a person dedicated to his trade. For, as I was to learn more fully, the builder who fawns on an architect's plans, however accurate and imaginative these may be, is a charlatan. A true builder despises architects. He despises them because, as MacLeod put it to me:

"An architect doesn't know that a 2-by-4 has length."

The importance of knowing that 2-by-4's may be bought in different lengths (and at different prices for each length) was something brought home to me later when I paid the bills for lumber. Wastage of wood – the bits and chunks sawed off – can be as high as twenty per cent in the roughing in and finishing of your rooms.

But, beyond this, what our carpenter meant was that architects are visionaries, not really of this world and therefore a cross to be borne by those who do the actual work. It is a tenet among tradesmen that the training of the architect should include a period of apprenticeship as a carpenter, plumber, bricklayer and like trades, so that his primary concern with aesthetics can be related to the practicalities of labor and materials. Unfortunately the architect would be sixty years old before he could start his career. Hence the dichotomy of construction that can remodel the homeowner's stomach by adding a couple of ulcers.

Because he must arbitrate between two strong-minded individuals who are polarized as the idealist (the architect) and the pragmatist (the builder), the homeowner will require all his resources of tact. He must act as a buffer, mitigating the collision between the concept of the poet who has prepared the drawings, and the facts of life that wear a hard hat.

Before engaging in renovation it is not a bad idea, therefore, to ask your friends and relatives for their frank opinion as to whether you have the wisdom of Solomon combined with the finesse of a career diplomat. If the consensus is that your flair for conciliation ranks you with a bull in a china shop, it may be as well to join a religious order that requires the vow of silence – at least till the plumbing is in.

The architect and the builder are of course fully aware of the degree of esteem in which each holds the other's viewpoint. They are accustomed to finding themselves in bed together, so to speak, and can adjust to one another without real discord. But when the homeowner jumps into bed between them, and becomes the object of their separate powers of seduction, he has a very difficult time hewing to the line between impartiality and seeming to be frigid.

He must judge each point of disagreement between architect and builder without fear or favor, then blame the decision on his wife. Since most architects and builders are married men, they understand that a wife's decision does not reflect the merits of the argument pro or con. It is like an act of God. More than once I said to the architect/builder:

"I agree with you, Ray/Wilf. But Myrl, well, ha, ha, you know how women are."

About half-way through our renovation both the architect and the builder discovered that my wife had sounder judgment than I had, and that her decision represented a legitimate score against one or the other. After that it was my wife who said:

"I agree with you, Ray/Wilf. But Eric, well, ugh, you know how writers are."

The implication was that they could not expect too much in the way of decision-making from somebody who was making a career of the male menopause.

From the point of view of the work on the house, however, the policy was sound in that neither the architect nor the builder lost face during our association. *I* lost face clear down to my ankles, but this after all was what I was paying for. The homeowner who prides himself on putting the architect or the builder in his place will find that he has paid an extra $2000 to enlarge his ego.

He has conditioned the architect and the builder to agree with him when he is wrong instead of disagreeing with him when he is right (the sign of a truly sincere relationship). In this respect we were fortunate enough to have a painter, Arthur Allday, so concerned about putting our welfare ahead of our pride that he adamantly refused to paint one room the color we had chosen. This is the mark of the ultimate in sound rapport with a tradesman: when he refuses to go ahead with the job at all.

If you complete your renovation without hearing a critical comment from the people engaged in it you may be reasonably sure that not only has the emperor no clothes but his palace has developed a boil on its buttress.

None of these home truths was known to me when I invited Mr. Olsen to meet Mr. McKnight so that they could appraise one another. The architect toured some of the builder's earlier projects, both renovations and new houses. It is sound policy for the homeowner to be as inquisitive as possible about the builder's track record. Contractual safeguards provide no real security. The only genuine protection you have is the tradesman's pride in his work, as evidenced in previous jobs. It is tempting to overrate yourself as a good judge of character, and although you can tell a good deal about a builder from his handshake, there can be a differential of several hundred dollars' worth of grief in the pressure of a pinkie, undetectable to the novice. Unless the tradesman actually has a halo poised over his head – with no wire visible when he removes his hat – it is advisable to check out his work other than the meticulousness with which he clips his mustache.

Ideally you will find a builder whose previous job was the restoration of a church steeple, of solid stone, in return for an honorarium of home preserves from the ladies' auxiliary, and the blessing of the minister in concert with the congregation.

More likely your contractor's earlier renovations will not be of an order to qualify him for sainthood. When inspecting these, the homeowner should keep in mind that the owner of the house he is snooping through will express himself as well satisfied with the work, even though the addition has developed some of the structural failings of a duck blind. Nobody likes to identify himself as a loser, so it is up to you to judge for yourself whether he is genuinely happy with the new patio whose drainage has provided him with the only sundeck in the world with a shallow end and a deep end.

Other anomalies to watch for:

A blue complexion of residents can mean that the existing heating unit was unequal to the task of warming the addition. Be suspicious of a cheery blaze in the fireplace, particularly if the mail slot has been boarded up to conserve heat.

If the taller children in the family appear dazed, it may be as the result of chronic concussion caused by insufficient altitude of the olde English beams that the builder has installed to enhance the renovation.

Ask to use the new bathroom, so that you can learn whether or not the added plumbing has attenuated the water pressure. If the toilet flushes a cloud of dust, it is safe to assume that the pipes are over-extended.

You should also check to find out how well the contractor was able to synchronize the performance of the various trades. The meshing of the work of carpenter, roofer, plumber, electrician, heating man, insulation crew, tile setter, stucco men and painter, plus the delivery of their materials, is an exquisite piece of orchestration. Only the contractor who knows his various sub-trades, and has won their confidence in his own timetable, can bring off the continuum of work on the project to keep the total elapsed time down to months rather than millenia. Everything devolves from the worth of the contractor.

The homeowner may of course sign with a builder who does only the framing (carpentry) while the homeowner engages each of the other trades on his own, or has his architect do this for him.

This is the recipe for chaos.

By the time he has finished trying to coordinate the services he is employing, the homeowner will have become accustomed to many, many days when the only sound heard in the uncompleted work is his own heavy breathing.

There is no substitute for the contractor who has been in the business of building whole houses – preferably large houses too well built to return him the profit he deserves – in the same locality as your house. The tradesmen will respond much more readily to him than they will to you, unless you have got to know them by repeatedly renovating your house, over the years, as a means of mortifying the flesh without breaking the skin.

Having applied these tests to the past performance of the McKnight Construction Company, without uncovering cause for alarm, and with the concordance of the architect, we moved to the point of no return: the signing of the agreement.

Compared to putting your name to the legal agreement with the contractor, the ceremony of signing the wedding contract seems like casual doodling. As the date set for the signing drew near I was tortured by all the pre-conjugal doubts of the bride. Was Wilf really sincere? Was my father supposed to supply the liquor for the reception? After we were united, the builder and I, would I prove to be a disappointing helpmate – useful in the bedroom but no good on the roof?

"Stop crying yourself to sleep every night, for God's sake," Myrl comforted. "Just think about how pretty you'll look."

How can you expect a wife to understand? After all, this was my first renovation.

7 I Do—But Does the Bank?

It was a quiet affair. Just members of the immediate family.

The ceremony was held in our dining room, architect Olsen officiating. He read aloud to the builder and to me the terms of the agreement he had drawn up. I may have blushed a little when he named the date on which the builder would take possession of the site.

The reading aloud, clause by clause, was helpful to me because I was not previously aware that the consummation meant that I had to increase my fire insurance. The architect urged that I pay the premium on the adjusted insurance right away, in case the house burned down before the renovation was finished. Nobody threw rice.

The contractor was made responsible for taking out liability insurance to cover damage to people or property during the work. Although the tone of these clauses creates an atmosphere as festive as the alterations made on Pompeii by Mount Vesuvius, it is better to be safe, if sobered, than sorry when the honeymoon is over. The architect can earn his fee in this single function of drawing up the contract, and deserves a glass of spirits.

The method of payment stipulated in the contract was that of cost-plus-wages, the builder estimating the total nut at about $12,000. The only financial backstop for me was that if the final figure much exceeded $12,000 the contractor would look rather silly. I was prepared for him to look up to $2000 worth of silly, and judged him to be the type of man whose tolerance of looking silly would never be greater than $3000.

Because of the psychological importance of the silliness factor, the homeowner should always ask for an estimate of total cost, regardless of whether or not the builder is contractually bound to the amount. And having obtained the estimate he should make a point of repeating the figure three times during the signing ceremony, so that it is duly witnessed. In our house we formed The Twelve Thousand Club, the figure embroidered on the girls' ponchos, printed on wall pennants, etc.

I even toyed with the idea of putting the announcement in the newspaper: "Mr. and Mrs. W. Nicol announce the engagement by their son, Eric Patrick, of Mr. Wilf McKnight, contractor, whose estimate of the job is $12,000 repeat $12,000."

The other major risk in the contract was the specifying of the date on which the work was to commence: January 6th. The possibilities opened up by removing the roof in the middle of winter did not deter the builder, but I could not entirely dismiss from my mind a bleak Currier and Ives picture of our family sitting down to dinner in the drifts of a blizzard swirling down from the ruptured roof. It was not my idea of a topless lunch.

For several nights after signing the agreement, instead of chasing my wife around the bed with lusty cries and slaps of the polythene phallus, as was my wont, I lay staring at the ceiling, seeming to see already the dark bulge spreading as the weight of ice built up for the terminal avalanche.

To be buried alive at a Swiss ski resort has a little class to it. The same could not be said of the circumstances described in the newsstory headed ALPINE RESCUE TEAM PROBES NICOL BEDROOM FOR BODIES.

Neither wintry setting nor uncertainty of final cost is as chilling, however, as the bath you can take in financing the project.

Some homeowners prefer to borrow the money to pay for the new construction, using their equity in the original house as collateral. This can result in the common syndrome of feeling that the ground floor is yours but the upstairs is haunted by your bank manager, compared to whom the shade of Jacob Marley was Mr. Sunshine. Because, if for some good reason you are unable to meet the payments on the second mortgage, strangers may move into the main floor, cutting you off from access to the ground unless the house is within leaping distance of telephone wires.

We decided against erecting the Great Pyramid of mortgage, that glittering epitaph to any hope of owning the house outright before we were moved into the pine prefab.

Instead we raised the wind for the renovation by displacing an amount from savings into a special bank account, operating on the simple principle that when the money was all gone, work would stop. Regardless. If that meant that the new plywood floors were naked of rugs, tant pis. Doors without knobs, tough titty. I stood with Polonius ("Neither a borrower nor a lender be"), though it might mean being unable to afford an arras to be stabbed through.

This method of financing, namely drawing on the family savings, presumes that you have some family savings on which to draw. The trick here is to start saving as soon as the third child is known to be on the way. Seven years later you have saved enough money to be able to move him out of the linen closet and into the new room. You will have done this by eliminating frills, such as friends, holidays, clothing, meat and other non-essentials.

We did so little entertaining during the years of saving that preceded our renovation that our first guest, aside from close relatives, was in fact the architect, one of several reasons why my wife got carried away and hung onto his legs when he was leaving.

The fact that we were pillaging our old-age security was something we made well known to all the trades. In this regard it is difficult to overemphasize the importance of first impressions. When the plasterer, for instance, comes into your house and finds you sitting in rags and gnawing turnip greens, he is going to be influenced in reckoning his bill.

Tradesmen are not, however, readily deceived. They will engage you in a political discussion, to determine whether your poor-mouthing is but a sham and you are in truth a Conservative who admires the Swiss tax system. Your becoming a Marxist for the period of the renovation, perhaps going so far as to hang a portrait of Lenin over the mantlepiece, depends entirely on whether your tradesmen are unionists. The rugged individualist, such as we had on the job, will not moderate his bills merely because your children raised clenched fists in salute when sitting down to their lunch of dry toast.

You should run your ghetto as a seven-day-week proposition. For instance, one Sunday morning our builder dropped in to pick up some tools and caught Myrl preparing a large roast of beef. Quick thinking, I identified it as horse meat.

"Really not bad, once you get used to it," I told Wilf. "The butcher said the cut was from a horse that had been ridden by an elderly jockey."

Such tactics are largely negated if you have two or more cars in the family. Fortunately we had only one car, a six-year-old compact. When tradesmen arrived in their sporty hard-tops, vans or pick-ups, I engaged them in conversation about the latest innovations in motoring that they enjoyed. ("Automatic transmission? That's where you don't have to crank the engine, isn't it?") I also rode a bicycle a good deal during the remodelling. Mine is a very old, one-speed bike, and I like to think that the pathetic squeal of the brakes, as I returned from making another withdrawal from the bank, struck into the conscience of the workmen.

A last word of advice about paying bills: I found it useful to set aside a special chequebook, with its own code for numbering cheques (SOB-1, SOB-2, etc.). This simplifies keeping the tally and provides a false sense of confidence in controlling the outflow.

8 The Primary Incision

Almost exactly nine months after architect Olsen had taken us under his constructional wing, builder McKnight and carpenter MacLeod arrived in their Datsun half-ton and unloaded the instruments required for the lobotomy on our roof. The shingles were only four years old, one reason why Myrl asked me if I wanted a local anesthetic as the power saw sliced through the outer sheathing, through shingle and shiplap, penetrating the skull of the house and exposing the ganglia of electric wiring.

We were committed.

The hole was for the purpose of admitting lengths of lumber into the attic, the other method being to carry the lumber through the kitchen and hall to the opening in the closet. Unless you have worked out some funny burlesque sketches involving two men carrying a ten-foot length of 2-by-6 through your breakfast, the hole in the roof is the more humane way of intravenous feeding.

Coincident with the holing of the roof came the first delivery of lumber. For some reason I had conceived the amount of lumber needed for the job as a small pile, readily accommodated in the potting shed. By the time the crew had finished stacking timber of various dimensions on my back lawn, we appeared to have single-handedly decimated Canada's forest reserves. Even without opening the back door we could feel the alarm radiating from neighboring houses, waves of hostility building to the cry of "Surf's up."

If you too are thinking in terms of a small pile of lumber, man, you're on a bummer. Nothing can be built with a small pile of lumber, not even a brick outhouse. This is why lumber manufacturers are so wealthy. Before the most benighted native of Africa can rebuild his hut of mud and cow-dung, a truck lurches out of the jungle and drops a load of No. 1 grade on his potatoes.

Because lumber is very expensive stuff, the manner in which the contractor orders it is highly relevant to your budget. If he orders from your neighborhood lumber yard instead of direct from the mill, you can add a couple of hundred dollars to the tab. Our contractor was a consummate master of the art of the scrounge, bringing to his dealings with the mill some of the finest qualities of an Arab slave trader bargaining for a selection of odd-length houris.

This does not mean that you should settle for less than No. 1 grade lumber that is as dry as possible. Green lumber, it should be noted, does not *look* green. That is, the branches and needles have probably been removed. But the water content is such that, after the lumber has been built into the house, it begins a spectacular career of shrinkage. The shrinkage is accompanied by the house's cracking its knuckles, rifle shots that jackknife you straight up in bed and provide many years of the sensation that you are trapped in the building with a mad sniper who also makes the door jambs sticky.

If the lumber is less than No. 1 grade, it not only shrinks but splinters, if shown a nail, in a jagged line that appears to trace the route of Marco Polo. It can warp not only lengthwise but in all other known dimensions including several usually observable only at seances. This makes for floors whose undulating surface adds to your wife's vacuum-cleaning some of the thrills of a roller-coaster ride – fun so long as you don't have to take a seasick pill before running to the phone.

Well-weathered carpenters insist that today's No. 1 grade lumber is equivalent to yesterday's No. 2, and today's No. 2 is little more than uptight sawdust. It even burns crooked. The old 2-by-4, which for some time has been 1¾-by-3¾, has lately shrunk to 1½-by-3½. Other sizes of lumber are similarly emaciated, the greed of the spruce budworm apparently being insatiable.

If therefore your builder brings along a trailer-load of old lumber that he has salvaged from earlier demolitions, especially beams and other heavy timbers such as went into houses built fifty years ago, the appropriate gesture is to fall on your knees and kiss the hem of his apron. I threw all the gardening tools out of the shed to make room, under cover, for the vintage 2-by-10's that our builder would use as joists under the new flooring. Whatever other shortcomings we faced in the upstairs, a trampoline floor resulting from immature underpinning would not be one of them.

As a gardener who takes some small pride in the condition of his grass, however, I went into mild shock at the descent of several thousand board feet of lumber on my back lawn. Although it was winter, the ground was not frozen enough to deaden the pain. For several months, each evening after the crew had left, I darted out to move part of the stacked lumber from point A to point B, to give the grass a chance to breathe. A few nights later I lugged it back from B to A. This routine, often executed in the dark, must have struck the neighbors as odd. For the carpenters, the erratic odyssey of the pile of lumber around the yard must have been even more inexplicable, and may have encouraged one of the helpers to give up drinking.

As for me, besides my finding it pretty exhausting, my wife became a little miffed at my coming to bed with chronically pitchy fingers. I think she considered me to be a fire hazard.

The homeowner whose garden is precious to him should therefore take note early in the proceedings that he is going to have special problems in maintaining a lawn and beds that are not naturally resistant to the kind of wear and tear associated with the passage of the Allied armies through Normandy. If planting bulbs, annuals and shrubs, he should choose those varieties that like lots of lime (in the form of old plaster), wood chips, nails and bits of asphalt shingle. A Japanese garden, composed of pebbles and blasted dwarf pine, is best adapted to house renovation, or better still you can discover the beauty inherent in a gravel pit.

Regardless of how he adjusts to the remodelling of his garden, the homeowner must be prepared to learn the names of various types of lumber used in construction. Otherwise, there will be a breakdown in communication with the crew when he attempts to describe what fell on the milkman's head.

First, the 2-by-4 (alias 1½-by-3½). The 2-by-4 is the work-horse of renovation. It is also the saw-horse (see chapter on blood sports). In Britain the 2-by-4 is known as a 4-by-2. Maddin, our carpenter, tells the story of the Englishman who went to the Canadian lumber-yard and asked for a 4-by-2. The attendant said:

"You mean a 2-by-4. How long do you want it?"

"Oh, for quite some time," replied the customer. "I'm using it to build a room."

The other stalwart dominating the rough stages of framing is shiplap. If you are not familiar with shiplap already, you will be before many moons have risen over the yard-arm. Renovation is indeed an education in names rarely heard outside the building trade, all of them sounding like characters out of a rather bawdy Restoration comedy – The Raking Line, or My Love Is a Fully-Louvred Bifold.

In addition to Sir Harry Shiplap (R.N.), the other characters of this play (definitely not suitable for children and people who rent) are Lady Bargeboard, married to a high station and the lover of Ridge Piece, a loose fellow, who bribes Soffit, the undercover agent, to make life difficult for his rival, Squire Rising Beam, whose servant Lintol is enamored of Mistress Mullion, who stands at the casement window and costs a leg.

Finally, there is Plywood, without whom this rollicking production would never get off the ground. It was a large sheet of plywood that on the third day of work slid off our frosty roof and crashed through the window of my den, launching the cat into stationary orbit over my desk and sprinkling me and the typewriter with siliciferous stardust.

Flying glass was not however the main reason why I subsequently became one of the few authors of light pieces to wear a hard hat when writing. As I tried to explain to my mother, who tends to fret easily, the headgear was primarily intended as protection from the fallout of sawdust from the little holes in the acoustic tile of the ceiling over my desk. At the end of a full day of hammering and sawing on the roof directly overhead, I had been emerging from my den looking like King Lear as made up for an amateur production – locks powdered preternaturally white, body wracked by manic sneezes.

Besides the hard hat you may wish to buy a set of ear protectors of the kind worn by airport groundcrew who guide jets to their loading bays. Living in a house that is being subjected to demolition and construction is an experience difficult to describe, but you can try to imagine being a mouse trapped in the percussion section of the massed bands of the Highland regiments of Scotland. I didn't buy a set of ear protectors because I was expecting a phone call (I am always expecting a phone call). In consequence, for four months I vibrated visibly, and I attended a rock music concert as a tranquilizer.

I was trying to write a stage play during this period, a sex comedy, but somehow every scene developed as part of the Battle of Britain. Each time my lead male character jumped into bed with the lead female character they were both obliterated by a direct hit. It thinned out the laughs, no doubt about it.

My wife and I tried to keep our morale up by starting a family betting pool: Which wall of the house will collapse first? Our young son, who had not got the model car racetrack he wanted for Christmas, found a substitute in watching the cracks in the plaster race one another around the walls of the living room.

The sledge-hammer treatment also quickly revealed which wall and ceiling fixtures had been insecurely attached. Hall light-shades, framed pictures, chunks of cornice, curtain-rods – they all crashed to the floor, making us aware of hazards we had been living with, ones that would not otherwise have been shown up unless we had an earthquake of .7 or greater on the Richter scale.

In addition to going to bed mesmerized by a swaying light fixture, the homeowner should note that exciting things are also happening *outside* the house, as old pieces of roof plummet to the ground. Your children will be bringing home schoolmates to watch the spectacle, and may charge admission. God knows you can use the money, if they can be bullied into sharing it, but the gain must be weighed against the chances that a neighbor's child will be brained by falling debris. If the child belongs to a neighbor whose view is being diminished by your addition, his readiness to laugh off the skull fracture is further reduced. In all conscience, the renovator should maintain vigilance against unauthorized persons within twenty feet of the perimeter of the house. (I found that a steady lope, clockwise, at one rpm, helped to keep the area clear.) Or you can buy more liability insurance and learn to ignore the sight of blood.

9   Protocol of Receiving a Trade

I lack the morning coat, striped trousers and topper, but otherwise our renovation qualified me for a post with any diplomatic corps in the world, including the Japanese, who can bow very cleanly from the waist. The homeowner who is not sensitive to the protocol of receiving tradesmen, who become more numerous as soon as the new roof has been sheathed, will see his blunders reflected in the workmanship.

I *Hours of reception.* Most tradesmen, being self-employed, start work as early in the day as possible. By arriving at 8 a.m. (or before) and working till 6 p.m. (or later), they can cram a year's employment into six weeks and have the rest of the year free to go fishing, hunting or travelling abroad.

It is necessary for the homeowner to be up and about when a tradesman arrives (see section II below), and he should not really go to bed till after they have left. It goes against the basically Puritan conscience of the North American to be eating breakfast when the carpenter has been at work for an hour, or consuming dinner while the same carpenter is still banging away upstairs. It takes all the flavor out of your fishcakes.

For me the adjustment in life style was particularly rigorous, as it had been my custom to wander around the house in my dressing gown till as late as 10.30 a.m. Writing at home, I found that up to mid-morning the creative impulse was limited to contemplating various methods of getting back to bed. My muse is a slattern with working hours appropriate to the prostitution of talent that I call a career.

Suddenly, I was getting up at 6.30 a.m., breakfasting in that hour of darkness, getting dressed and sitting at the typewriter by 7.45 a.m. Not writing. Just sitting. Staring with glazed eyeballs at the blank sheet of paper that drew nothing, absolutely nothing whatsoever, from my still-numbed brain. My fingers lay on the typewriter keys, twitching spastically, and whenever a workman passed by my window I typed furiously: "Now is the time for all good men to throw up."

Despite these heroic measures I did not fool our builder. An experienced contractor is as resourceful as a trainer attending to a stunned football player on the field: he will ask you your name and address and confirm that you are out on your feet.

Here I should draw attention to the fact that it is impossible to know on what day a specific sub-trade, or group of sub-trades, will arrive to start work. The sequence of events characterizing the materialization of a sub-trade is as follows:

(a) Appearance by sub-trade contractor, who sizes up the job, after dark, on weekend, etc. Often vanishes before you can get your dental plate in.

(b) Appearance by rival sub-trade contractor, who scents the spoor of the first sub-trade contractor and deliberately knocks the loose mortar off your chimney.

(c) Return of first sub-trade contractor, to talk to your builder, who may introduce you if he thinks it will do any good. As a rule, he doesn't.

(d) Arrival of truck with material. Truck driver and helper unload material in place you have designated (where your spouse parks her/his car).

(e) Arrival, on time, of the workman whose job it is to find that the truck has delivered wrong material. Workman leaves after ten minutes, is never seen again.

(f) Some time while the whole family is out, truck picks up wrong material, deposits correct material where you park *your* car.

(g) A day earlier than expected, at 7.30 a.m., crew arrives and cuts off your water. This means that work has commenced.

II *Conveniences.* Aside from learning to love the sky at dawn – an acquired taste, in my opinion – and making an impression of pro-letarian unity, the homeowner has to be up to unlock doors so that the tradesmen can get in. After a few weeks the builder will have installed his own door, upstairs, with its own lock, both accessible from a ramp and exterior scaffolding. Thereafter the first intimation you have that it is time to get up is when a stranger walks past your bedroom door carrying a tool case.

This can of course affect the homeowner's sex life (see section III, *Sex during alterations*). But his first thought should be for the needs and comforts of the workmen. This means unlocking both back *and* front doors. A few, though not many, of your labor force will be sensitive to any insinuation that the tradesmen's entrance is other than whichever door has a red carpet run out to the sidewalk.

Similarly, in the matter of washroom facilities:

(a) If you indicate to the crew that they are to use the bathroom in the basement, make sure that they have access other than breach-ing the concrete foundation. You should also use the same bathroom yourself, democratically, after everybody else has. Better still, be seen easing springs behind the privet hedge. Brotherhood is all.

(b) Tell all members of the family to clear the approaches to the master bathroom. The builder will not use it, but he will have a young apprentice who has yet to master the skill of containment. This man has the right of way at all intersections.

(c) Make sure that all bathrooms (if any) have at all times an adequate supply of toilet paper, even though you and yours are reduced to using Saranwrap.

III *Sex during alterations.* It is quite possible that the nervous strain imposed by renovation of your home will render you temporarily frigid. If so, count yourself lucky. The opportunities for careless rapture, or even careful rapture, that goes beyond a bit of hasty slap-and-tickle with the carpenter's T-square are sharply reduced.

The main factor in quelling the libido is the sudden and unannounced arrival in your bedroom, via door, window or straight through the ceiling, of persons to whom you and your bed-mate have not been formally introduced. Also the scaffolding erected outside the window provides semi-permanent bleachers for peeping Toms, realtors, stray cats and other nocturnal creatures.

You may find that intimacy is excited by such esoteric foreplay as when you and your mate find an old bottle of paint thinner that saves your painter a trip to the wholesaler. The fierce embrace stimulated by saving six dollars an hour plus travelling time can get out of hand. Watch it. It is also strange that a man and a woman should be drawn to one another by mounting an extension ladder together, but the temptation to fool around is obvious to anyone familiar with the moral climate of a hayloft. Looking up, on a ladder, can be as perilous as looking down.

It seems like something of a hardship, for a couple married fifteen years, to have to climb into the car and drive to the nearest lovers' lane in order to neck. But if the renovation has been occasioned by your having more children than you can accommodate, it will strike your workmen as irresponsible if they come upon you making love before the addition is even completed.

Plasterers and stucco men, usually being Italian, are broad-minded about catching the homeowner and his wife in flagrante delicto, but your stone mason, a Dutch Calvinist, may feel that you have let his hod down, rather badly.

To summarize: renovating your house may increase your experience of coitus interruptus. If this type of birth control is contrary to your religious beliefs, you should seriously consider selling.

IV *Other tools.* In addition to playing host to a considerable number of working people, your house will be providing accommodation for their tools. Tradesmen often leave their tools – power saws, ladders, paint brushes, etc. – while they go home for lunch, or even overnight if you have no previous record of pilfering.

On no account touch a workman's tool.

You will be tempted, and your children will be very tempted, to pick up and examine a particularly exotic-looking wrench. Don't. It will fall to pieces in your hands. Life holds few moments more dismal than that when you stand holding the dismembered remains of an electric drill belonging to the carpenter and worth at least sixty dollars.

That the drill was ready to fall apart is irrelevant. The fact to be absorbed by the homeowner is that all tools, and especially those costing a hundred dollars or more, are built so that metal fatigue reaches critical mass at the exact second when the tool is picked up by a hand belonging to your immediate family.

Therefore any time you find a workman's tool left on the premises, even though it is sitting in the middle of a busy traffic area such as the kitchen table, treat it like an unexploded bomb. Throw up some kind of screen around it. Top the enclosure with barbed wire. And post a notice: MINED TOOL – KEEP OUT. Despite these precautions the tool will be found broken, if it is not missing altogether, when the workman returns for it. But at least you can point to the evidence of a good try, before you make out the cheque.

In this regard it should be noted that when several trades are on the job at the same time they occasionally *take each other's tools.* One aluminum ladder looks much like another, but only the homeowner looks guilty. This is one feature that the architect can do little about: the aspect of the man who is using the remodelling to re-stock his home workshop. All the homeowner can do is pray that it is not a four-ton truck that goes missing. Be it ever so humble, his home, in the eyes of the trades, is still large enough for him to hide pilfered objects of any size.

Finally, you may expect the various trades to borrow *your* tools. They do this for a variety of reasons. Sometimes they lack the tool themselves, but more often they like to use your tools just for a change, or a chuckle. Wilf and Maddin enjoyed borrowing my tools, because the tools were so archaic that they were sort of a challenge, as it might be for a modern prairie farmer to plough with a charred stick.

The box of tools that my father-in-law had given me right after the wedding contained some rare old specimens. The tools had belonged to "Uncle Bill," an elderly gentleman who boarded with my wife's family and who dropped dead when I started courting Myrl. His tools included a screwdriver with a Gibson Girl wooden handle and a leather-jerkined tape-measure that appeared to be marked off in ells and perches. The weight of the brace and bits suggested that they had been extracted from the same rock that yielded Excalibur.

While making sure that his tools are fit to lend, the homeowner should make sure that he knows what tools he has.

"May we borrow your hack-saw?" Wilf asked on one occasion, when the team was feeling nostalgic for bygone eras.

"I don't have a hack-saw," I said.

"Yes, you do," said Wilf, producing from my tool box what I had taken to be a medieval instrument used by midwives.

On the other hand my stepladder, which I knew to be such, the crew eschewed as having more sway than an overweight belly dancer. They told me to buy a new stepladder and to lay in a good supply of cardboard boxes, the kind without holes in the sides. These were for the carrying out, by me and other members of the family, of each day's production of wood chips, sawdust and general debris.

This rubbish was supplementary to the main disposal, into a rented box the size of a railway freight car, that was dropped into our driveway and remained there for several days like an exaggerated version of the basket used to catch the head of the guillotined. To meet the demand for cardboard boxes in which to carry out rubble, after the freight car was hauled away bulging with our old roof, shingles and gutters, my wife had to change supermarkets.

At the height of the demolition we were filling an average of three cardboard boxes a day with rubble, mostly broken plaster. Hence the need for physical conditioning before you start renovation. From the first lengths of lumber to the final swatch of floor carpet, you are going to use muscles that have been unemployed longer than some parts of the Maritimes. Having a handsome new staircase loses something if you have to be carried up it for the rest of your life.

Your fitness program should give emphasis to weightlifting and karate (you don't want to have to *saw* all those odd lengths of wood to fit the fireplace). Running through staggered tires placed on the ground – a basic drill for football players – is also excellent preliminary to trying to answer the phone during renovation.

I was not in as good condition as I should have been, to tote rubble, according to the medical specialist who has recommended a spinal fusion to enable me to stand erect again. My problem was compounded by the error of piling the cardboard boxes of rubble on the patio, where they got rained on. When I had something like thirty boxes built into a pyramid that would not have disgraced King Tut, and I tried to carry them to the lane for final disposal, the soggy bottoms fell out of every box. A moving glacier of gunk crept back towards the house, a monstrous surge threatening revenge for the havoc wreaked upon hallowed walls.

"More cardboard boxes!" I yelled to my wife, grabbing a shovel.

My wife roared away in the car and returned with a dozen cartons of fancy-grade asparagus. It meant eating asparagus nightly for the next five years, but we stemmed the terrible tide of litter.

Bribing the garbage men to accept the additional overburden was another expense not included in the original estimates. Not all of the garbage men had the same taste in beer, necessitating research into their favorite brand of suds as well as the laying in of supplies. The weekly visit of the garbage truck was attended like the arrival of the first brides' ship, because if we missed it the debris overwhelmed us. The cry, "Truck, ahoy!" sounded from the crow's-nest upstairs brought all hands tumbling to the cardboard boxes, while my wife broke out the lager and ale. Spirited moments, and more were yet to come.

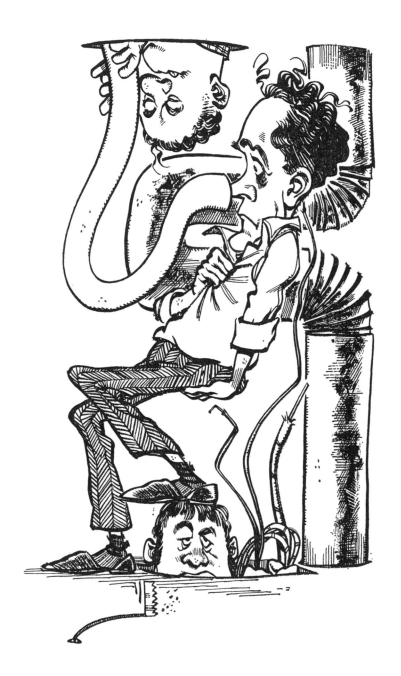

10 Donner and Blitzen and Wasser

One thing rarely mentioned by magazine articles on home remodelling – perhaps because the subject is too intimate for a family publication – is the adjustment to your ducts. Unless your basic accommodation has been a stone cave, it is already serviced for heating, wiring and plumbing. If you were to take a cross-section of your house (and if you don't somebody else will), you would see that it is a network of conduits of various sizes, none of them disposed to relate to the new addition.

This is why one day you hear a new laugh added to the chuckles of the regular crew up top. It belongs to the sheet metal man. He is looking for places to bring heating pipes into the new rooms without shafting a sofa. Before he arrives, however, you will have done a good deal of research on central heating, starting with Dante's *Inferno* and reading on.

I *Home comfort.* The oil companies call it Home Comfort and offer the services of an expert to size up your addition and tell you, down to the last degree of frost, how uncomfortable your home is going to be with the added load imposed on your old furnace.

Having confirmed that this service was free and without obligation, I invited an oil company to despatch a heating expert to analyze our problem. Part of the problem was that I was not sure that we *had* a problem. I tried to convey this aspect of the problem on the phone to the oil company, but we were disconnected.

The TV commercials had conditioned me to expect a fellow dressed like Sherlock Holmes and trailed by a bumbling Watson. I needn't have bothered wiping the fingerprints off the thermostat. The heating expert arrived dressed conventionally in a blazer and grey slacks, and he was not noticeably amused by my request for a selection on the fiddle.

He explained that it would be necessary to make a study of the heat-loss factors (windows), correlate these with the total floorspace to be comforted, and measure the result against the output of the existing furnace in B.T.U.s. As one who till recently thought that B.T.U. was an eastern U.S. college specializing in arson, I did not grasp the entirety of his exposition. He did not appear to be surprised at my failing to comprehend. Very tired, yes, but not surprised.

"Will the old furnace do?" I asked.

"Ah," he said. "That's difficult to say."

"No, it isn't," I said. "Will the old furnace do? See, I said it again."

"I'll leave you my card," said the heating expert, retreating towards the front door. "Call me when you've made up your mind."

"About what?" I said, but he was gone.

Later that week I phoned the number on the card, but the oil company's home comfort station said that the expert had not checked in for several days and did not answer his home phone. I got the impression that he had emigrated to the tropics, where the heat-loss factor was negligible.

If the home comfort expert is quite definite about your furnace being unequal to the task of heating the new rooms in addition to the old, you may consider ways of supplementing the wheezer laboring in the basement. This we did.

I have always coveted electric heating because one of the basic premises of my hypochondria is that fossil fuels discharge an exhaust that is at least partly to blame for my shortness of breath, the shrinking of type-face in the telephone directory, eczema and whatever else is currently defacing the picture of health. I found, however, that electric baseboard heating, highly recommended by hydro corporations, can be installed at a moderate cost that sometimes causes the homeowner to overlook the fact that his light bill will leap upward by as much as twenty per cent, depending on how often his wife lies naked on the bearskin rug. It is cheaper to wrap yourself in an electric blanket every time you go upstairs, even though it means buying five hundred feet of extension cord.

Radiant heating and hot-water heating are two other exotic ways of preventing the formation of icicles on the end of your nose. Again, the only kind of radiant heat I could afford was that of filling the space between the wall studs with old Playboy calendars. As for hot water, the cost of putting in the additional furnace needed to warm it on its way made my blood run cold, cancelling out any benefit.

When he saw that I was resigned to the fact that there is no fuel like an old fuel, our builder called in his own sheet-metal man, whose well-worn coveralls bespoke many years' experience in spit-balling the capacity of the distended octopus below stairs.

"Hell, yes," said Bill, gauging the furnace against the length of his cigar. "She'll cope easy."

Money can't buy that kind of judgment. It can make a down

payment, yes. But the wages of intuition based on a lifetime of actually embracing furnace pipes are love, and faith, and a little something special at tea-time. (See Appendix A, recipe for Sheet-metal Man's Snickerdoodles.)

The sheet-metal man's only problem was that of finding places to hide the new pipes from the furnace to the rooms being added upstairs. We could of course have taken the pipe straight up through the middle of the new bedroom, pasted French posters on it and passed it off as a kinky kiosk. But it can be hell on the metatarsals in the dark.

The problem was complicated by the facts that (i) fan-driven hot air prefers to travel more or less continuously upward, rather than by way of Cape Horn, (ii) today hot-air registers are placed on outside walls, usually under a window. All our old registers were on inside walls, a geriatric humilation of which we had been unaware till enlightened by the home comfort expert. One of the emotional adjustments that one must make, during renovation, is learning to live with one's old hot-air registers. The best way to do this is to screen them off with potted plants that thrive on warm, dry winds: desert palms, cactus, sagebrush, etc.

Introducing the new furnace pipes therefore involves "cheating." This differs from the better known type of cheating in that instead of taking a mistress you take a corner of a linen closet here, and an alcove containing the family's lares and penates there. It so happened that we had the sheet-metal man and the plumbers all cheating on the same day. They kept running into one another in cupboards, fouling up each other's cheat.

The plumbers decided to concentrate their cheating in my den, where I was working. The first I knew of this was when I saw a saw excising a hole in the ceiling, like a Bugs Bunny cartoon, above my bookshelves. While I hurriedly piled books into boxes, the plumbers cheated right down behind the knotty cedar panelling above the den fireplace, where they ran the sewer pipe for the new bathroom upstairs. I had a good view of the versatility of the plastic sewer pipe, which compared to old-fashioned iron pipe is as sinuous as anaconda.

While I was admiring the new sewer pipe over my fireplace I was horrified to see another serpent, a small orange one, slithering upward along the pipe. I had forgotten that the electrician and his helper had also chosen that morning to cheat a little.

II *More power to you.* The mob scene – all we needed was Charlton Heston directing traffic to have the makings of a biblical epic – was a benign type of confusion. Being able to cheat ensemble, and coordinate their use of holes cut in the floor and ceiling, the sheet-metal man, the plumbers, and the electrician and his helper (many hands make light work) established a togetherness that helped to reduce the number of perforations. Again, a credit to our builder.

The orange power cable was strapped to the new sewer pipe, and the cedar panelling restored with no bother other than my being crowded into a brief suspension from a drapery rod. This was the only improvisation the electrician was required to make, the placement of lights, switches and outlets in the new rooms having been specified in the architect's drawings. Once the floors and wall boards and ceilings have been nailed home, it is extremely awkward to ask for a ceiling light for which there is no switch, or to find that the only outlet in the room is so situated that every time you want to vacuum clean the room you must first crawl under the bed to plug in. If you are not employing an architect, before the electrician comes it is a good idea to have a dry run of all possible uses of lights, switches and outlets, even though this means that the neighbors see you straddling skeletal framework with a hair dryer on your head.

Our architect providently placed a light switch on the wall between the placement of the twin beds, so that in the event of hearing a strange noise, such as that of an intruder, in the en suite of the en suite bathroom, I could turn on the light therein without having to remove my head from under the pillow. *That*, in my opinion, is thinking ahead.

If you suspect that you may sometime need an air-conditioner upstairs, have the electrician install the wiring for it, as the machine usually takes a voltage different from that of the other fixtures. After pricing air-conditioners my plan for keeping cool in summer boiled down to acquiring a large palm frond and hoping to meet a giant Nubian who felt that Lincoln went too far.

The greatest service our electrician, Guy, rendered us however was that of correcting the neural disorders developed by our house over a period of thirty years and all treated by my gingerly stuffing a wad of tinfoil into the socket.

On the wall of the kitchen my wife had scotch-taped the sign: DO NOT USE TOASTER AND DISHWASHER AT SAME TIME. To the owner of a newer home this message might have seemed occult and slightly Hebraic, a commandment against the browning of bread in the time of the passing of water.

Actually the sign related not to a higher power but to the lower and diffuse one that blows fuses. Our house was long in the tooth but short in the wiring, as was confirmed, years before we renovated, by the electrician whom I summoned for a second opinion after the first electrician mutely crossed himself and walked away.

As I understood it, the house had plenty of outlets but not enough inlets. With the acquisition over the years of electrical appliances that were not even a gleam in the inventors' eyes at the time when the house was built, we developed the situation where certain combinations in the use of juice caused a fuse to go pfft.

In our house a fuse went pfft on the average of twice a week, plus matinees on Saturday and Sunday. The hardware store that supplied us with fuses gave us a special rate by the gross, and every year the fuse manufacturer sent us a nice Christmas card picturing Santa Claus plugging in a Christmas tree. The card blew out our dryer.

Besides the signs posted by my wife, the full list of regulations, which was distributed to guests and the day workers who stayed on the job about a half-day each before the juice got to them, was as follows:

1. We switch off the TV set before turning on the back porch light.

2. The playroom has only one electrical life support system, and this is why there is a miner's lamp attached to the vacuum cleaner.

3. Mother uses her electric razor between spasms of the refrigerator. Otherwise her Ronson defrosts itself.

4. That all the electric clocks in the house show the same time means nothing if anybody has used the waffle iron.

5. All overnight guests will kindly submit to being frisked for electric toothbrushes. They are also warned that if they want a hot bath they must refrain from using the sewing machine for at least half an hour before they turn on what they think is the bathroom light.

6. On absolutely NO ACCOUNT is the record player to be plugged in during winter months when the furnace is operating. The last time we heard the LP of "Peter and the Wolf" two persons went to hospital with frostbite.

These were the simple rules of living in a house that didn't have enough amps in its plans. The electrician who told me that it needed rewiring spent some time admiring the complex fuse boxes that occupied most of one wall of the basement. He wanted to buy – for its historical value, I gathered – our main electrical switch, which could not be thrown till we had reeled in the kite.

Guy replaced these archives with a trip-type box that incorporated the multiplicity of cables writhing against the ceiling. I was persuaded to accept this extra expense not only by the aesthetics of the unified source of power but also by the fact that the building inspector would have condemned any exacerbation of the Laocoon Group.

The only chronic ailment that resisted rewiring was our doorbell. The doorbell is a rather elaborate choir of gongs that for the original owner played any of three different musical selections, the only survivor of which was "How dry I am." Over the years the "dry" had desiccated itself so as to be inaudible. The doorbell played "How ———— I am," a vaguely obscene refrain that became excessively obnoxious when the carpentry upstairs caused wires to get crossed and the doorbell played "How ———— I am" for the better part of an hour, till somebody seized an axe and severed the nerve.

III *Lady Chatterley's plumber.* The homeowner, in the act of renovation, does not establish a truly durable relationship with his plumber, compared with the emotional ties he weaves with his carpenter and his electrician. For one thing, there are long intervals between appearances of the plumber, and, for another, when he does come, the plumber and his helpers spend much of their time running up and down stairs or secluding themselves in a bathroom, where their activities are too arcane to invite interruption.

This does not mean that the plumber fails to make his presence known. I found that, when they install new fixtures, plumbers produce a special wrench, larger than the rest of their wrenches, and perform on the toilet a symbolic rite known as Beating The Shit Out Of It.

This ritual makes all previous and subsequent noise of construction sound like The Pastoral Symphony.

Only after the plumbing has been thoroughly intimidated do you begin to appreciate that the plumbers bring a touch of pornography to the remodelling. It is a fair treat, overhearing their remarks about male and female couplings, about nipples and cocks and whatever turns you on. If you are too shy to buy a copy of Fanny Hill, the next best thing is to eavesdrop while plumbers install your drains.

Among other facts of life I learned what was the purpose of the small pipes that protrude from the roof and appear to have no function other than complicating the retrieval of your child's kite. Our new plumbing had to be connected to these minor stacks, the hot-water pipes to the smaller ones, the sewer pipe to the larger, in the interest of avoiding an explosion. It was news to us that our house had been exhaling sewer gas all these years. I thought it was me.

Our local building regulations required that this exhaust pipe be at least ten feet from the nearest opening window. Apparently there is danger of marsh gas or something seeping into your bedroom, and you may not want to sleep in the same room with an expendable canary.

These are points worth remembering when planning your remodelling because, though Santa Claus comes down your chimney only on Christmas Eve, there's no telling when the building inspector will climb down your throat via the sewer vent.

I therefore shook hands feelingly with the plumbers, as they departed, grateful for the thoroughness with which they had reconstituted the house's viscera. And as I resumed my place at the desk in my den, somebody upstairs flushed the new toilet for the first time, releasing the spillway of Grand Coulee right over my fireplace and causing the cat to rise, once again, straight up to the ceiling. I was a little hurt because the new addition had been baptised before I could make the ceremony.

11   Finishing Touchy

Towards the end of the second month of renovation some of the camaraderie, the will to endure, begins to wear thin. By this time the builder will have made several ad hoc decisions, with your approval, in the architect's absence, that the architect on his weekly visit does not entirely approve of. He is only partly mollified by your taking full responsibility for the deviations, because he knows by now that you don't have much of a mind of your own.

Conversely, the architect will have been shown to be merely mortal, his drawings overlooking a couple of structural problems that the builder has greeted with a soliloquy that would have to be omitted from the school edition of the drama.

In this situation the homeowner must again draw on his reserves of tact if he is to spare all hands embarrassment. He will, for instance, make himself scarce when the architect inspects the work of a tradesman, if the tradesman is still on the job. The discussion will not gain from his presence, ears flapping to fan any latent indignation into open hostility. My own policy, after welcoming the architect at the door, was to excuse myself while I went out to the shed and got lost in the peat moss.

Once or twice I was nearly trampled by tradesmen who had seen the architect coming and suddenly decided that they had a dental appointment.

Despite these adjustments you will be forced to make on-the-spot decisions, when the architect and the builder, or the builder and a tradesman, or all three, confront you with their opposing recommendations regarding the choice of a material, or the positioning of a stairwell light, or the shaping of a hand rail. You will in fact be faced with approximately 620 such decisions, at least half of them instantaneous, with a man aiming a blowtorch at your parquet. If you are constitutionally incapable of making a decision, without first consulting your church minister or a psychiatric social worker, renovation is not for you. The final, unplanned phase of remodelling will be the installation of stout bars on the windows, to contain your classic case of locomotor ataxia, and you will be moved around on castors.

Forced to the wall – one of the first uses to which that new surface was put – I backed the judgment of the architect. I did this for three reasons:

I Hiring an architect and not following his advice is like consulting a doctor, then changing his prescription.

II The architect is trained to see the unity of concept, to reconcile the parts to the whole.

III Our architect told us not to make any decisions without informing him first, and he was bigger than I was.

Once or twice I was tempted to ignore I and II, but there was no hurdling III.

In spite of his massive effort to help us with minor decisions as much as he could, Mr. Olsen had to leave some of these to us. This is how Myrl and I confirmed – as we had long suspected – that we had no taste. No taste whatsoever.

Fifteen years earlier, when we bought the chesterfield suite that was our first item of furniture, the salesman offered to send out the store's own interior decorator, free, to fertilize our decor by artificial insemination. But I had always identified with those self-reliant people who believe that they can inject their own personality into the interior decorating of their home without the assistance of an alien.

"No thanks," I said, shaking my head and causing some of the rocks therein to shift slightly. "We're looking forward to expressing our own taste in the furnishings."

"Ah," said the salesman, and he glanced up and down the blue sports jacket I was wearing with my brown pants. "Should be very interesting."

So we went ahead and decorated the living room red and green – "warm, fundamental colors," as I told my wife, "because there is nothing pastel about our personalities."

Besides the green chesterfield and the red chair and the other green chair and the red hassock, we assembled furniture in a variety of styles that an artist friend of ours described as a successful wedding of the traditional and the berserk.

We had an old English chair and a modern Danish coffee table that were fighting one another with a vigor unmatched since the days of Ethelred the Unsteady.

Our collection of pieces in mahogany, walnut, oak, teak and imitation maple, which at first seemed to us a harmonious concert, gradually took on the aspect of a museum exhibit: Woods of the World.

We then moved most of the living room furniture and drapes into the basement, or my den, and began over, this time in consultation with stacks of home decorating magazines. I was pretty sure that we had grasped the contemporary decorative principle of juxtaposition of apparently uncongenial colors, such as brown and blue. I also seized on the new names for decorator colors, buying a "toast" chair and a "cinnamon" cushion to put on it. Cinnamon toast, get it? Ho, I said, why import a pantywaist aesthete when your brain is teeming like this?

After a few months of living with the new decorator colors my wife looked at the chesterfield one day and said: "All it needs is a throw."

"What kind of a throw?" I said.

"Up."

With this kind of background in decorating the intelligent person calls in an interior decorator to plan the details of his new addition. Myrl and I fought off our intelligence, however, instead sitting down evening after evening to a dining room table piled high with samples of wallpaper, of bathroom floor tile, of bathroom shower tile, of Arborite (and its younger rivals Wilson Art and Formica), of carpeting, of charts of paint colors. Every evening we got up from that table certain, yes deep-down convinced, that we had every bit as much flair for interior decorating as a chimpanzee tossing pizza into an electric fan.

Yet we refused to concede. We went ahead and made our own choices of everything, clearing the way for the dangerous kind of panic that immediately set in: having lost all confidence in our own judgment, we started soliciting opinions of every selection in decor. We started with relatives and friends, but as the rot set in deeper we resorted to anybody that we suspected had some sense of style – neighbors, the delivery man for The Bay, brush salesmen. One time I had to restrain my wife from buttonholing a complete stranger passing our house. (His jacket seemed to complement his trousers, we thought, and she wanted to take him into the new bathroom for a look at the roll of wallpaper.)

For the male homeowner this stage of the renovation can inflict psychological damage well beyond his loss of faith in his sense of *le bon ton*. The man who has regarded himself as essentially masculine, possibly on the strength of playing rugby scrum half and receiving an honorable discharge from the armed services, finds himself agonizing over the choice of a soap-holder for the bathtub. Embroiled in more and more decisions about things called "accents," his lips budded poutily from the recurrent effort of helping a room to make its "main statement," he is apt to overcompensate. He tries to reassure himself about himself and the way he walks, by loping up and down the stairs two at a time – very dangerous on raw treads with no hand rail.

I forget exactly when it was – somewhere between the selection of door knobs and the shopping for bathroom lights – that I deliberately gave up the deodorant and tried to drop my voice an octave. For several weeks I came across as a Popeye whose spinach had withered. When my wife and I went into yet another department store's rug department, I put one foot up on a bolt of shag, jumped a pack of Marlboro out of my vest pocket, and squinted into the near distance as if I knew that the herd was headed for the broadloom.

Besides raising doubt in your mind about latent sexual perversion of the old man, this stage of remodelling is laced with disappointments when you learn, after the tortured effort to decide on an item of interior decorating, that the number is not in stock and must be ordered from a firm in Logy, Alabama, that is currently strikebound.

Because of this hazard you should choose alternatives of every material, trying to stay loose about your preference. A woman can accept the evidence that she is living with a fairy, but being denied the window blind she has set her heart on can really hurt. Myrl and I learned to spread our lack of taste over a range of second and third choices. Because the third choice is always in stock, we sometimes pretended that the third choice was our first choice, in which cases the second choice was in stock.

We also had to make a compromise in the matter of the hand-rail for the comely staircase our builder had completed. He had saved us a goodly sum by using two-inch plywood for the treads, as solid as ordinary wood, and no less attractive when covered by stair carpet. But the hand-rail was something else. Thousands, probably millions, of people have slid down hand-rails without giving a thought to the cost of shaping and installing the rail and banisters. (Some don't even know that it is not possible to slide down a banister, because the banisters are what your baby will get his silly little head stuck between unless your architect has taken care to specify openings either too narrow to admit the youngster's bonce or wide enough to let his whole body fall through and be done with it.)

No two staircases being exactly alike, in pitch, number of treads or spiral conclusion, banister and hand-rail must be tailored to measure. Using wood, which objects to curving around corners, this can be murderously expensive. The newel alone can play The Last

Post over your budget. Sometimes the homeowner can salvage a newel from an old building that is being wrecked, but such is the competition for these valuable antiques that he may run into a rousing battle redolent of The Three Musketeers, if one imagines D'Artagnan leaping onto a lady love in order to defend his staircase.

We had to settle for a hand-rail and banister of what has been called overwrought iron. Our architect was very firm about keeping the design of the rail as plain as possible, gently quashing our natural inclination towards the New Orleans Vieux Carré bordello style of ironwork. But the two-inch cap of the railing, curved at the bottom of the staircase, proved to be a trying experience for the ornamental iron men accustomed to working with stylized flamingoes and lacy leaves.

"We'll have to bring in heat," they said, then wheeled across the threshold an enormous oxygen tank from which dangled a very black, vicious-looking torch. It takes large reserves of cool to see, and hear, your front hall turned into Hell's own blacksmith shop. The volume of smoke pouring from the front door activated the concern of neighbors, to whose enquiries our young son explained: "Our house is in heat."

The hand-rail had to be hack-sawed and lugged back to the shop several times for reshaping, and the whole project began to take on the monumental proportions of the building of the C.P.R.'s transcontinental railway. My wife cried openly at the ceremony of driving the last spike, and for weeks after the heat had been trundled away for the last time, if we placed a hand on the rail we seemed to feel it tremble with the approach of an operating deficit.

Until I paid for these accessories to levitation, I thought of a staircase as something you took when the elevator wasn't working. It may well be that this cost factor is one that you can ignore. If you can afford a staircase on the order of the celebrated double spiral in the Chateau of Chambord, the magnificent stone convolutions that permitted François Premier and his courtiers to chase the ladies up and down stairs without knowing whether or where they would run into one another, the price tag on the finishing stages will not rock you.

As for me, I was stunned to learn that a simple chrome latch for the new bathroom window cost $3.50. As with the staircase, it had never occurred to me that being able to open a window was a luxury.

Our builder was able to buy many of our items of hardware

from the supplier at a reduced price. Even so, it was extraordinary how quickly the bill for minor items such as door hinges and cupboard handles threatened to exceed my annual income. The make-or-break point lies in the exercise of phenomenal amounts of self-discipline when you are choosing hardware yourself, in whatever store offers the widest selection. You will see displayed ornate brass door knobs worthy of the papal palace, baroque t.p. dispensers, clothes hooks so superb you are obliged to throw out your entire wardrobe to avoid disgracing them. Be strong. Shake off the mesmeric appeal of orchestrated lamps, gilded and pendant, that will turn your bathroom into a festival of *son et lumière.*

If possible, lash yourself to a friend to whom you owe money. Like Ulysses, plug your ears against the siren song of the medicine cabinet whose mirror is also a music box ("Stay As Sweet As You Are"), against the Scylla of the whirlpool home sauna – "The family that steams together, teams together."

Our architect had specified solid doors for all the new rooms. He was old-fashioned enough to want to feel weight when he opened and closed a door. The solid thunk of a door is another expensive luxury these days when the door core is commonly vacant enough to yield to a huff and a puff from the Big Bad Wolf's grandmother. We settled for semi-solid doors: heavy enough to allow us to close the bedroom door with a sense of being shacked up in a motel that at least had AAA approval.

The installation of any kind of door, like other elements of the finishing phase of renovation, will take longer than you anticipated. It even takes longer than the builder anticipated. Indeed it is doubtful that Divine Providence, peering into eternity, did not underestimate the duration of the process of hanging a slab of wood on a set of hinges. The reason for this is that it is much easier to hang a man than to hang a door. Hanging a man is a matter of slinging a rope over a beam, kicking away a chair and Bob's your uncle. Hanging a door, on the other hand, can take hours, possibly days, if the right type of hinge is unavailable, which it normally is.

One of the longer selections of dramatic dialogue that I have been audience to was that between Wilf and Maddin positioning a door from opposite sides of it.

"You come to me."

"Too much. You come to me."

"No, you'll have to come to me."

"Easy. Your bottom out a bit more."

"How's that?"

"Beautiful. Come to me a little."

"Too much. Come back to me an inch. . . ."

The spiciest door scene since "What The Butler Saw." But when the craftsmen are so conscientious, the running time is longer than that of the unabridged "Hamlet."

Another work comprising many long scenes, some of them bloody, is that of buying rugs for your new rooms. There is a tendency to minimize both the importance and the cost of floor covering, and to postpone a decision till the day when the carpenter nails down the last sheet of plywood and stands waiting to be told how much clearance to leave under the doors.

Every door must be cut so that it swings over the rug without either scalping it or leaving a gap through which the winter drafts will whistle cool jazz. Today's rugs offer variations in height of pile from a half-inch seisal to as much as three inches of elephant shag or more if you are covering your floor with wolf hide or a hobby-craft drugget of pubic hair.

The time to start looking at rugs therefore is several weeks before you think you need to. As a rough guide to relative virtues of wear and appearance, rugs start with the costly elegance of wool and descend, in quality, to nylon, acrylics, polyesters and cotton. The choice here is schooled by budget, but nylon shags are very practical, we found, as well as merciful to the matinal foot seeking solace for emerging from the sheets.

Myrl and I came to fancy ourselves as pretty adept at judging the quality of rugs, by measuring the number of tufts to the square inch, noting the twist of the yarn and the strength of the backing. Some manufacturers dye the backing the same color as the fibre in order to camouflage the fact that the pile is as sparse as the beard of Dr. Fu Manchu. Take along a ruler with you to the store, and don't be afraid to dig your fingers into the broadloom. The clerks will respect you for it, as you can tell by the alacrity with which they run to ask if they may be of assistance. When I plucked at a floor sample with my fingernails, to test how the rug would stand up to the cat, the salesman was moved to offer to throw in a pound of liver, to expedite the sale.

Another point about buying rugs: remember that a rug is only as good as its underpad, and it is poor policy to pay sixteen dollars a yard for your Windswept Glory, then underlay it with the roll of felt your son picked up during the Scouts collection.

The underpad plus the charge for laying the rugs will add perhaps twenty-five per cent to the cost of the rugs. Never skimp on the hiring of a professional carpet layer. There is no such thing as an amateur carpet layer. There is only the professional and the poor, gibbering wretch permitted to pad his own cell.

Almost as pregnant with disaster is the laying of floor tile. Here the hazard is the new, improved cement with which the homeowner, regardless of good intentions to the contrary, becomes involved. It doesn't seem possible that a scrap of wet tile, discarded by the tile setter in the bathroom, could find its way into the liquor cabinet downstairs, where it glommed onto fingers fumbling for the medicinal nightcap. Yet this is precisely what happened to me. Like the helicopter seeds of the maple tree, bits of gluey tile will travel incredible distances in order to fulfill their destiny down your jockey shorts.

I found that this tile cement is so new and improved that when you get some on your fingers you can remove it only by:

(a) amputating the finger to the nearest knuckle (the simplest and most efficient method), or

(b) using a pumice stone. An ordinary pumice stone will not touch it. You must abrase your finger with a special pumice mined in the mountains of Morocco by hard-core convicts armed with diamond-bitted jackhammers. Even after you have pumiced your finger sharp enough to pick locks, you will still be able to smell the residuum of glue, an odor that disappears roughly two weeks after cremation.

It is possible, of course, to avoid this digital adhesion by putting carpet on the bathroom floor instead of tile. Much depends on whether you have a small son whose trajectory is spirited but erratic. We chose tile.

Tile-cement sniffing, inhalation of glue and lacquer thinner – these are unavoidable perils of the final stages of renovation. They are especially dangerous to couples who are practising planned parenthood but haven't really got the hang of it. It takes only a few minutes of holding the light while your wife spreads paint stripper on the laundry bins, in the confined space of the utility room, for both of you to start hallucinating like billy-o.

I don't wish to invite controversy about the morality of indulging in mind-expanding guck in the privacy of your own laundry bin. No doubt a case can be made for seeing the plastic slop-bucket as a psychedelic and even ineffably religious experience. But unlike a normal head hooked on mucilage, the home renovator is usually unaware of what is happening to him and/or her. Sometimes it is not till the following morning, when they find that they have slept together in a driftwood shelter hastily fashioned from lumber lying around the back yard, that they realize that they should have used a longer-handled brush.

Dangers of glue-sniffing aside, you are well advised to leave the laying of Arborite and similar materials to people who specialize in this work. We had the old tile of the kitchen counter replaced with decorative laminate, and learned what happens when the homeowner fails to remove the drawers and empty the cupboards that lie immediately below the demolition of the old tile: he finds his Revereware full of rubble, gravel in his griddle, and his flour bin beefed up with enough roughage to keep him regular beyond the wildest dreams of Big Ben.

Our painter moved into the kitchen before we had time to excavate the drawers. It was during this period of *angst* that there arrived in town from Toronto a magazine editor whom I was anxious to impress favorably, and whom I had earlier invited to have dinner with us during his visit. The smart thing to have done would have been to take him out to dinner, but a sudden gust of house pride blew me into bringing the editor home.

My wife was giggling when she opened the front door to us, a sure sign that her normal state of distraction had received an extra boost towards out-and-out hysteria. I soon discovered why: the team of carpet layers had arrived and were still hard at work stapling rug to stairs and main hall. Scrap ends of acrilan lay convulsed on every thoroughfare, the aroma of freshly cut synthetic mingling with the smell of paint.

The painter left during the soup, but the carpet layers worked right through entree and dessert and coffee and well into the evening. I wouldn't have minded the reverberations from their staple gun so much, but during lulls in the firing their conversation was more interesting than the one I was able to muster with my editor guest. I strongly suspected that while I was out in the kitchen desperately replenishing his glass with shale, he took the names and addresses of the carpet layers as possible contributors to his publication. As for me, I received no assignment, and I cannot help relating this silence to that occasion of cutting a rug without the joy that is dance.

Conclusion: if it is true that people who live in glass houses shouldn't throw parties, it is equally true that the homeowner in the middle of remodelling should entertain only those people he wants never to see again.

12 Ascension Day

It's eerie. The silence.

One day, they are all gone. The carpenters and the electricians, the carpet layers and the stucco men – suddenly they have left.

No more, the painter's lunch-bag in your fridge. Mute is the power saw, its strident song sung elsewhere. The coffee pot sits on the hob perking poignantly, cups waiting for lips that never come in.

For the first time in months, you and your spouse are alone, truly alone.

You may enter any room of the house you want without first asking permission from a pair of coveralls. You must adjust, mentally, to the possibility that the phone ringing is for you, rather than for the tradesman whose wife is calling to find out how late he is going to be for supper.

Even the paint in the halls is dry, so that you no longer have to carry the children from the back door to their rooms, and vice versa, to keep their fingers off the final coat of the expensive egg-shell-stippled off-white. It is a magic moment, only slightly tainted by your finding in a closet the little pile of bleached bones that reminds you that the cat too had its routine disrupted.

Like the bird that has been kept in a cage so long that it cannot accept the freedom to fly beyond the opened door, the homeowner may experience the trauma of a kind of catalepsy: he is unable to make the actual move upstairs. Unless quick action is taken he can become permanently petrified in his old den downstairs, clutching the emaciated chequebooks that represent payment of the bills (for us, the total was $16,196.56, including tax*), and blinking only when the sun shines directly into his eyes.

The only remedy for this condition is, quickly, to break out a bottle. Regardless of the time of day, the entire family should have a good stiff belt straight from the jug. Be graceful about the official opening of the addition, if you can, or as we did crawl upstairs on your hands and knees. The main thing is to crack the psychological block to living ten feet nearer to God.

For it is truly a spiritual experience, to stand hand in hand with your loved ones, and gaze out the new upstairs window, and know the transcendent joy, the uplift, of being able for the first time to look down on neighbors you have had to look up to.

* Also including repainting of whole house, inside and out, rugs, drapes, lamps and marriage counsellor.

There they are, getting ready for bed, in *their* upstairs room. Wave to them. See how delighted they are to see that we can see that they can see that we can see them. Give 'em the old choke-up sign. They'll love it.

Everybody – not just the kids but everybody – should have an upstairs room. To escape the foul vapors exhaled by the ground, yes. But more important, to be renewed by a view of the horizon that expands to the periphery of the soul, so that when you go to bed the blood responds to the ambience of visible stars, to trees hushing the wind to be still.

I have never wanted for excuses to delay coming to grips with the typewriter, but my new study upstairs has provided dilatory reserves that will never be exhausted in my lifetime. I have given up my office in the press building, a windowless cell so monastic that I was at times constrained to work, and now give myself fully, indeed with almost indecent abandon, to the savoring of sunsets that purple the farthest hills, or to that indefatigable wardrobe mistress Nature shirring cotton clouds into a negligee for the moon.

I concede however that in terms of dollars and cents our renovation was an extravagance. The city tax assessor, who had been circling in the sky waiting for the last bill to drop, assured us that the increased value of our taxable improvements was well under the amount that we had paid out for the addition: Frigidaire should offer such cold comfort. Also, about the same time that we settled the last account payable, the bottom fell out of the seller's market for houses. For the same amount of money we could have paid the difference on a brand new house.

But we would have missed the experience of renovation itself. We would never have met, and learned to appreciate, the diverse qualities of Ray and Wilf and Maddin and their wives, Jim and Bruce and their girl friends, Guy and Bob and Joe and Arthur and their philosophies of life, which varied from Baptist rectitude to the expressed intention of using my cheque to play the blackjack tables in Vegas.

A renovated house is like a bride's ensemble: something old, something new, something borrowed (who can afford chairs?) and something blue (we are having a little trouble getting heat into the living room).

Myrl and I are immensely pleased with our renovation. We have to be. We can't afford to leave it, even for a minute. This year we are spending our annual vacation in Chateau country, Chateau being the name that Crane gave to our new loo. If Myrl so much as takes out the garbage, I run into the room she has vacated, expanding to enjoy it for both of us.

Instead of brooding about the amount by which you have exceeded your budget, we urge you to consider that, besides the new rooms, you have been left with:

enough sand to fill the childrens' sandbox and have ample remaining for a private beach;

enough kindling to last you 126 years;

enough odd-shaped pieces of drywall to create a giant jigsaw puzzle, to amuse elderly members of the family including you;

enough nails (assorted) to monopolize the market in your neighborhood for king-size mattresses for Indian fakirs;

enough fractionally-filled paint cans of different-colored paint to paint your own large mural, titled Erection No. 2.

The only criticism I make of home renovation is that the person who wants to have this cosmetic surgery done on his house has no guide-line of procedure, no general practitioner to whom he can go for referral to the specialists – the architect, and the contractor. The construction industry is being modernized by prefabrication and modular assembly, but the hundreds of people who own or have bought an old house and want to remodel it are babes in the wood yard, dependent on crumbs of information to lead them safely to the home of their dreams.

For those who enjoy the challenge of the Unknown, and who are too old to qualify for the crew of an orbiting space station, renovating the house is certainly fulfilling. Your new rooms up top are not just accommodation, they are a badge of courage – Through Adversity to the Stairs.

Happy landing.

Appendix A

1. Architect's English Tea Scones

2 cups sifted all-purpose flour
2 tablespoons sugar
2 teaspoons cream of tartar
1 teaspoon baking soda
½ teaspoon salt
1 egg
¼ cup shortening
⅔ cup milk
Sift dry ingredients into a bowl (china, not plastic, please). Beat egg without malice. Add milk. Combine with dry ingredients, stirring lightly to blend. Turn out on lightly floured board and knead gently 10 times. Roll or pat with hands to thickness of ½- to ¾-inch, and cut into rounds or squares.

Place on ungreased baking dish and bake in hot oven, 450° F., for 10 to 15 minutes. Makes 18 scones, or one very tasty manhole cover.

Note: Add 1 cup raisins to dry ingredients, if desired. You may use 4 teaspoons baking powder instead of cream of tartar and soda.

2. Builder's Cherry Bars

1 cup sifted all-purpose flour
¼ cup icing sugar
¼ teaspoon salt
½ cup butter or shortening

filling:
2 eggs
¾ cup brown sugar
¼ cup all-purpose flour
½ teaspoon baking powder
¼ teaspoon salt
½ teaspoon almond flavoring
1 tablespoon melted butter
½ cup chopped glace cherries
½ cup fine coconut
½ cup chopped walnuts or pecans

Sift together the 1 cup flour, the ¼ cup icing sugar and ¼ teaspoon salt. Cut in butter until mixture resembles coarse meal. Press mixture firmly into bottom of ungreased 9-inch square pan. Bake in moderate 350° F. oven for 10 mins. Remove from oven. Beat eggs slightly, add brown sugar, flour, baking powder and salt. Beat until well blended. Stir in butter and flavoring. Add cherries, coconut and walnuts. Spread evenly over partially cooked dough. Return to 350° F. oven and bake for another 25 mins. Cool in pan and, if desired, spread with a thin layer of butter frosting. Cut into bars. Makes about 36 servings, or one sitting for average-size builder.

3. Carpenter Coffee Cake

2 tablespoons butter
½ cup, firmly packed, of light brown sugar
2 tablespoons maraschino cherries, chopped
2 tablespoons chopped nuts
¼ cup well-drained crushed pineapple

filling:
2 cups all-purpose flour
½ cup sugar
2 teaspoons baking powder
½ cup butter
½ teaspoon salt
1 egg
1 cup milk

Cut 2 tablespoons butter into brown sugar. Stir in cherries and nuts, then lightly mix in pineapple, keeping mixture crumbly. Set aside as topping.

Sift together flour, sugar, baking powder and salt. Cut in ½ cup butter until mixture resembles coarse meal. Beat together egg and milk, add all at once to dry ingredients, stirring only until moistened. Pour into pan. Sprinkle with topping. Bake at 400° F. for 30-35 mins. (9-inch square pan). Serve slathed with butter, every hour on the hour till carpenter belches contentedly.

4. Sheet-Metal Man's Snickerdoodles

Mix thoroughly:
1 cup soft shortening (part butter)
1½ cups sugar
2 eggs

Sift together and stir in:
2¾ cups sifted flour
2 teaspoons cream of tartar
1 teaspoon soda
¼ teaspoon salt
Chill. Roll into balls the size of small walnuts. Roll with mixture of 2 tablespoons sugar and 2 teaspoons cinnamon. Place 2 inches apart on ungreased baking sheet. Bake until lightly browned but still soft. These cookies puff up at first, then flatten out. Bake for 8 to 10 mins. in moderate hot oven (400° F.). Makes about 5 dozen 2-inch cookies, small enough to be dropped down furnace pipe to sheet metal man working below.

This book was illustrated by Roy Peterson
and designed by David Shaw.